The Sutton Hoo Ship Burial

ANGELA CARE EVANS

Published for the
Trustees of the British Museum
by British Museum Press

Second impression 1989
Revised Edition 1994

Designed by Harry Green

Set in Palatino
Printed and bound in Great Britain
at The Bath Press, Avon

ACKNOWLEDGEMENTS

Fig. 3: British Library Map Room; fig. 4: Cambridge
University Committee for Aerial Photography; fig. 15: by
courtesy of Mrs Barbara Johnstone; fig. 56: by courtesy of
the Dean and Chapter, Durham Cathedral (B.11.30, f.81v);
fig. 93: drawn by James Farrant; figs 95 and 97: Statens
Historiska Museum, Stockholm; fig. 96: Universitets
Museum för Nordiske Fornsäker, Uppsala; fig. 98: Nigel
MacBeth; fig. 99: Mick Sharp. Quotations from *Beowulf* by
kind permission of Longmans.

FRONTISPIECE The burial chamber, 27 July 1939. Mrs Pretty
sits in her cane chair, looking into the excavation where
Stuart Piggott, W.F. Grimes, Sir John Forsdyke (Director
of the British Museum) and T.D. Kendrick (Keeper, British
and Medieval Antiquities, British Museum) examine the
shoulder-clasps.

Contents

Preface

The first *Handbook* was published in 1947 and has now been through several editions. 1984 saw the opening of a new exhibition of the most important of the ship-burial finds in the Early Medieval Gallery, as well as the first full season of renewed excavation on the Sutton Hoo site directed by Professor Martin Carver, University of York, with the support of the Trustees of the British Museum and the Society of Antiquaries of London, as well as many other bodies. These excavations ended in 1992 and the full report will be published within the next two years. However, some of the most important of the recent discoveries are presented in preliminary fashion in this new version of the *Handbook*, and the author and publishers are very grateful to Professor Carver and the Sutton Hoo Research Trust for giving their permission to include an outline of these discoveries in advance of publication. The revolutionary excavations of 1939 rewrote the early medieval history of England, and this latest campaign has gone a long way towards helping us to understand better the protracted history from the Bronze Age to the seventh century AD of this most extraordinary of cemeteries.

The author wishes to thank many scholars who have helped her with this guide: Rupert Bruce-Mitford, formerly Keeper of the Department and author of the first *Handbook* as well as of the major three-volume *The Sutton Hoo Ship Burial* (BMP, 1975–83); her colleagues, Katherine East and Susan Youngs, and among others Myrtle Bruce-Mitford, Elisabeth Crowfoot, Valerie Fenwick, Fleur Shearman and the late Nigel Williams. The line drawings are principally the work of Carey Miller, until 1985 the Department's chief illustrator. British Museum Press has throughout proved a most creative and helpful partner in this enterprise.

NEIL STRATFORD
Keeper of Medieval and Later Antiquities
March 1994

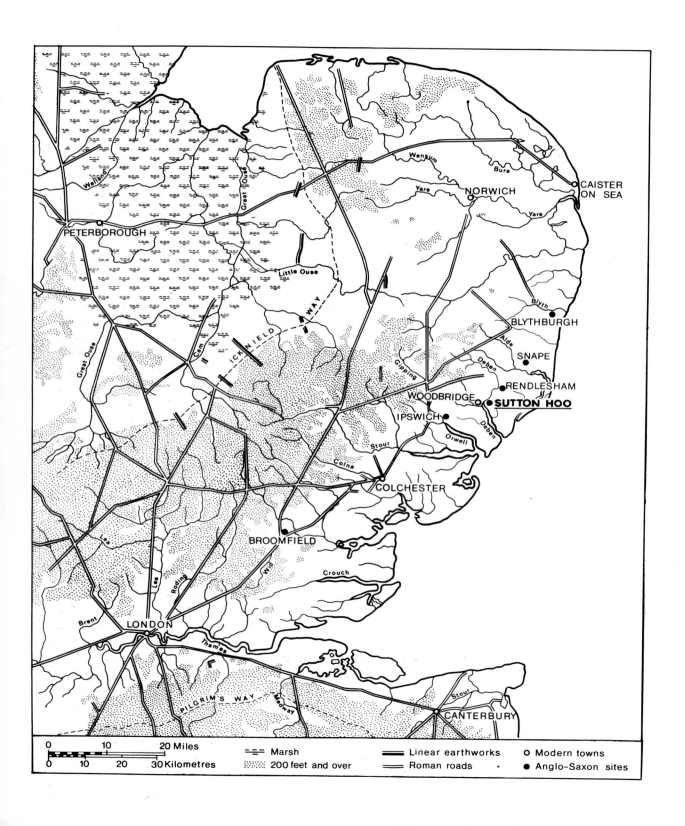

CAISTER ON SEA

PETERBOROUGH

Welland

Great Ouse

Little Ouse

Wensum

Yare

NORWICH

Bure

Yare

Blyth

BLYTHBURGH

Alde

SNAPE

ICKNIELD WAY

Cam

Gipping

Deben

RENDLESHAM

WOODBRIDGE

SUTTON HOO

IPSWICH

Orwell

Deben

Great Ouse

Stour

Colne

COLCHESTER

BROOMFIELD

Crouch

Lea

Roding

Wid

Brent

Lea

LONDON

Thames

PILGRIM'S WAY

Medway

Stour

CANTERBURY

| 0 | 10 | 20 Miles | === Marsh | ▬▬ Linear earthworks | ○ Modern towns |
| 0 | 10 | 20 | 30 Kilometres | ∷∷ 200 feet and over | ══ Roman roads | • Anglo-Saxon sites |

Introduction

1 Map of East Anglia showing Sutton Hoo in relation to other places mentioned in the text. The southern boundary of the East Anglian kingdom was probably made by the river Stour. By the middle of the seventh century Ipswich was a trading entrepot and an important centre for manufacturing pottery.

On the edge of the windswept plateau overlooking the estuary of the river Deben in Suffolk lies a group of low circular burial mounds – the Sutton Hoo gravefield. In 1938 the first of a long series of excavations began with the opening of three mounds. All had been robbed, but in 1939 the largest mound was excavated and a magnificent Anglo-Saxon ship-burial was discovered containing finds of remarkable wealth and unparalleled artistic quality. It is thought to be the grave of one of the seventh-century kings of the East Angles, perhaps Raedwald who died around 624/5. The finds included gold and garnet shoulder-clasps and belt fittings, a large collection of silver, a helmet with a formidably realistic face-mask, a large parade shield and a magnificent sword.

For two months newspaper reports with banner headlines kept the British public informed about one of the most remarkable events in twentieth-century archaeology until at a Coroner's treasure trove inquest the contents of the royal grave were awarded to the sponsor of the excavation, Mrs Edith Pretty, on whose estate the barrow group lay. In a gift of great generosity she presented the finds to the British Museum.

In late August 1939 the grave goods were moved from Suffolk to London and when war broke out they were stored, still in their excavation packing, in a tunnel off the Aldwych tube. In 1946 preliminary conservation and restoration of the most fragmentary objects began and archaeologists started to evaluate the find and its impact on both Anglo-Saxon and European archaeology.

In 1965 archaeologists returned to Sutton Hoo to re-open the ship-mound and to begin investigating the flat land between the mounds. These excavations uncovered a small group of unaccompanied burials and cremations and provided a glimpse of how the gravefield may have been used between the sixth and eighth centuries. The 1970s were chiefly devoted to publishing the 1939 finds but when this was completed a new phase of excavation began. This is designed to explore all aspects of the gravefield and its relationship to the kingdom of the East Angles and also to establish the history of the site back to the neolithic period, perhaps three thousand years before the Anglo-Saxon burial ground was established.

This work is still continuing and while the objects from the 1939 ship-burial form an integral part of the British Museum's Anglo-Saxon collections, the current excavations, with their prospect of greater understanding of the gravefield and its place in the history of the East Anglian kingdom, provide a continually expanding background against which the 1939 finds must be seen.

1 *The Early Excavations*

2 The stand that lay at the west end of the burial chamber is lifted, using a plank for support. In the chamber are W.F. Grimes, Stuart Piggott and Sir John Forsdyke, outside are Charles Phillips and T.D. Kendrick, with Basil Brown behind.

1 The Sutton Hoo gravefield

Relatively little is known about the history of the gravefield. The group of mounds was first recorded in 1601 when the cartographer John Norden produced a survey of the lands of Sir John Stanhope. On one of the sections is a representation of the barrow group where the mounds are shown as four humps that are confusingly similar to Norden's representation of the steep hill that rises from the east side of the road bridge up to the plateau. In 1629 a land survey of Sutton Parish was drawn up and on this the barrow group is again shown by four humps that are called Howhilles. In 1783 a one-inch-to-the-mile survey of Suffolk shows five mounds and the nearest group of buildings, at the foot of the escarpment below the gravefield, is called Sutton How. The mounds are first described as 'tumuli' on the one-inch Ordnance Survey hill sketches drawn in 1836. At the end of the nineteenth century the Ordnance Survey produced their first series of larger scale maps and on the six-inch sheet of 1889–91 the cemetery is shown with the ten largest mounds on the site.

On every map from 1601 the mounds are shown either straddling or immediately to the south of a road that led down to the river and they must have been a familiar sight to local travellers, yet they are not mentioned in any documentary source and they appear to have been largely ignored apart from their plundering in the late sixteenth century when only the depth of the burial chamber in mound 1 prevented it from being ransacked. The robbers dug straight down from the top of the mound and were only inches above the burial deposit when they stopped and lit a fire. It must be assumed that the walls of their shaft, which were well over ten feet deep, began to fall in, for they did not continue digging but abandoned the pit, leaving their fire

and a tiger-glazed Bellarmine wine jar. The robbing of the mounds has been associated with Dr John Dee, alchemist and court astrologer in the reign of Elizabeth I, who may have been given a commission to dig for treasure in East Anglia by the queen. There is however no evidence for him ever visiting Sutton Hoo and the robbing of the mounds in the late sixteenth century may be coincidental.

The cemetery suffered its first recorded 'dig' in 1860 when a mound was opened on an afternoon spree and two bushels of iron nails were found – and given to the local blacksmith. No mention of any finds other than the nails is made in the newspaper account that reported the dig, and this suggests that the mound had already been robbed. The identity of the barrow may be mound 2, the boat-burial which the archaeologist Basil Brown was in 1938 to describe as ransacked. The fact that he recovered only a handful of rivets from a boat which must have been built with several hundred would support this, as does the position of the mound just beyond the top of the coombe that contains the road leading up from the river. The 'excavation' was organised by a party from a naval survey boat that was in the process of recording the Deben estuary.

From the mid-nineteenth century until 1938 the burial ground remained in obscurity. Local reports suggest that at some time during the nineteenth century the heathland surrounding the cemetery and the slopes down to the river were ploughed, and far-sighted landowners established mixed plantations of conifers and broad-leafed trees to form windbreaks to prevent the sand blows that deplete the slender reserves of topsoil. No archaeological investigation of the cemetery took place until 1938, when the owner of the estate on which the mounds lay, Mrs Edith Pretty, decided to excavate them.

3 Detail from John Hodskinson's survey of 1783 showing Sutton Hoo (arrowed) in relation to the river Deben. The hachures indicate the steep rise from the river flats to the plateau on whose edge the cemetery lies. The Deben is tidal up to Wilford Bridge, its first road crossing.

Ufford
Melton Industry House
Brooke Esq.
Squerels Grove
Eyke
Melton
78
Rook Yard Farm
Bromswell
Wilford
Bridge
Part of
Hundred
WOODBRIDGE
77
Ferry Ho.
Quays
Sutton How
Hatchley Barns
Creek
Sutton Walks
W I L F
Hollesly Heath
White Post
Sutton
River Deben
Methers Gate
Stanaway Point
Pistree Hall
Wood Hall
Waldringfield
Chilton Hall
Shottisham Cross
Shottisham
Shottisham Creek
Hall

The gravefield today

4 Aerial photograph of the cemetery, showing mound 1 after excavation in 1968. The straight lines of the anti-glider ditches dug across the site during the war are still clearly visible (cf. figure 5).

5 Site plan showing the principal mounds. Mound 1, the ship-grave, was excavated in 1939; mounds 2, 3 and 4 in 1938. Mound 2 was re-opened in 1985. Several extremely low mounds have been recognised during recent surveys, bringing the total to 19 or 20.

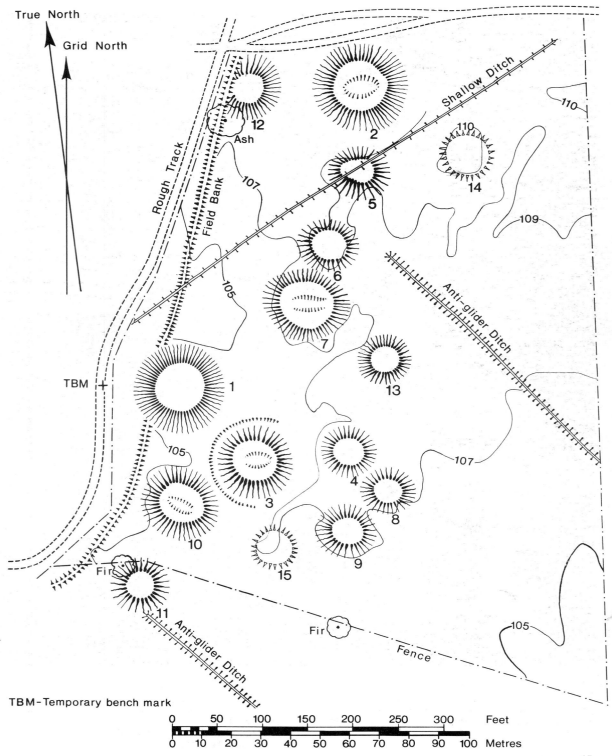

True North

Grid North

Rough Track

Field Bank

Shallow Ditch

107

105

110

109

110

14

Ash

12

2

5

6

7

13

Anti-glider Ditch

TBM

1

105

107

3

4

8

10

9

15

Fir

11

Anti-glider Ditch

Fir

Fence

105

TBM–Temporary bench mark

| 0 | 50 | 100 | 150 | 200 | 250 | 300 | Feet |

| 0 | 10 | 20 | 30 | 40 | 50 | 60 | 70 | 80 | 90 | 100 | Metres |

15

2 The first three mounds, 1938

Mrs Pretty had been interested in archaeology since visiting excavations in the Nile Valley in Egypt. Before investigating the barrows at Sutton Hoo she contacted Ipswich Museum and asked the curator, Guy Maynard, for advice on who to employ to open the mounds for her. He suggested a local archaeologist, Basil Brown, who had had many years' experience in working on the light sandy soils of East Anglia.

Brown's first task before beginning his excavations was to make a brief survey of the bracken-covered mounds, noting their surface condition and making a rough plan of the gravefield. On 20 June 1938, his first day on the site, he wrote in his diary that the mounds were considerably larger than he had anticipated and that he 'was rather alarmed by their size'. Brown selected mound 3 as the first to be opened after dissuading Mrs Pretty from mound 1 (the future ship-burial) because of the amount of disturbance that he could see on its western flank.

Mound 3 was a 'well-shaped mound ... of medium size ... that showed little disturbance other than rabbits'. It measured about 85 ft in diameter and stood about 5 ft high. He approached it by cutting a 4-ft-wide pilot trench into the mound on an east/west axis. The trench began outside the

mound on the west where it produced evidence of a shallow ditch. Towards the centre Brown encountered the first traces of pre-barrow disturbance which he interpreted as a pit. Brown set out trenches at right angles to his original trench to trace the limits of this disturbance and also opened up an area of 12 sq ft in the centre of the mound where he believed he would find the burial. Eventually, 5 ft below the old ground surface the first traces of a burial were encountered when a few fragments of bone were found. More cleaning revealed a disturbed burial deposit that had apparently been placed on a 'tray' or platform of oak which had largely decayed. The wooden 'tray' was aligned roughly east/west and measured 5 ft 6 in long and 1 ft 10 in across. On it lay two heaps of cremated bone from an adult male and a horse.

Towards the west end of the 'tray' Brown found several small decorated sheets of bone, perhaps the facings from a casket or a comb-case, and a piece of bone or ivory delicately carved with a scene that probably represented a winged victory of Roman or Byzantine workmanship. Nearby, and also of east Mediterranean origin, lay the cast bronze lid of a ewer

6 Plan and sections of mound 2, based on field plans made by Basil Brown in 1938.

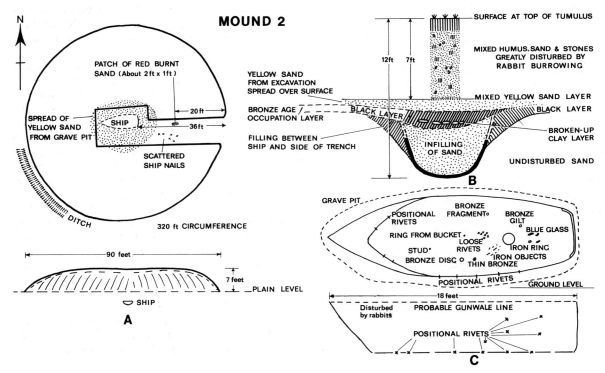

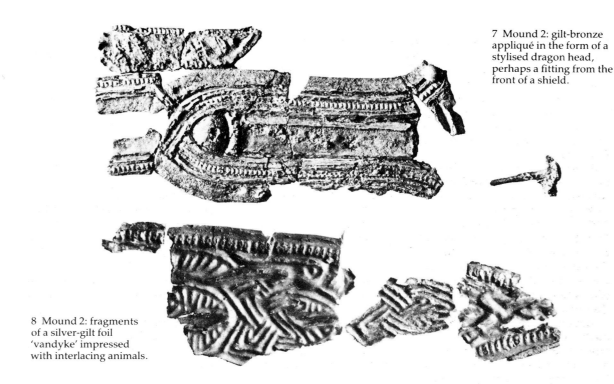

7 Mound 2: gilt-bronze appliqué in the form of a stylised dragon head, perhaps a fitting from the front of a shield.

8 Mound 2: fragments of a silver-gilt foil 'vandyke' impressed with interlacing animals.

9 Mound 2: gilt-bronze disc decorated with a complex design of animal interlace. The disc may be a shield fitting.

or jug, with a baluster handle and two links of a bronze attachment chain. Just beyond the southern edge of the 'tray' lay the heavily corroded remains of a *francisca* – a form of throwing axe.

After mound 3 Brown moved on to mound 2, which he approached from the east with a 6-ft-wide trench. The mound was a little larger in circumference and higher than mound 3 and appeared to have been much disturbed. The first sign of a burial came from the recovery of two iron rivets that lay in the approach trench, and further into the mound from a spread of clean yellow sand that lay over the buried ground-surface. Brown argued that this bright clean sand could be the upcast from a large excavation in the natural sand and he eventually uncovered a pit that was 20 ft long, 6 ft across and dug 5 ft into the natural sand. The pit was aligned on an east/west axis and narrowed towards its western end in a boat-like fashion and, although only a handful of rivets were recovered, Brown had no hesitation in identifying it as a boat burial, but see chapter 16 for a reinterpretation of this burial after excavation in 1984–5.

The grave, an inhumation, had been comprehensively robbed once if not twice and all that remained were fragments of the rich possessions buried with

the dead man. The most important finds were a
7–9 silver-gilt triangular mount from the mouth of a
drinking-horn and two gilt-bronze mounts possibly
from a shield. The tip of a pattern-welded sword
and four fragments from a squat blue glass jar were
also recovered, together with a small group of
fragments of once fine objects: a silver buckle, a
bronze ring with a flat attachment plate, fragments
of the blades of two iron knives and a scramasax,
part of a double sheath containing two knife-blades
set in opposite directions and the foot and fragmentary bands from an iron-bound wooden tub, similar
to the one found a year later.

After the ransacked boat-burial in mound 2, the
last, smaller mound that Basil Brown tackled in 1938
was to prove an anti-climax. Mound 4, only 65 ft in
diameter, was riddled with rabbit burrows and
showed signs of disturbance. Brown uncovered a
small centrally placed pit measuring about 7 ft long
by 3 ft wide and 3 ft deep. In it he found a scatter of
cremated bone, one burnt bone or ivory gaming
counter and small fragments of sheet bronze, but
little else apart from a few scraps of textile. It seems
that the cremated bones of a young adult and a
horse had been placed in a bronze container that
may have been wrapped in cloth. The textile scraps
are of high quality and amongst them traces of
feathers were found, which suggests that the grave
may have contained a cushion or pillow.

Although the three mounds opened in 1938 were
robbed of all but a few finds, enough survived to
suggest that they had once covered high-status
Anglo-Saxon graves of the mid-sixth/early seventh
centuries. They also produced evidence of different
rituals surrounding death, including boat burial,
something completely unexpected despite the fact
that an Anglo-Saxon ship-burial had been excavated
in the nineteenth century at Snape, only nine miles
north of Sutton Hoo. Although the results were not
spectacular they were enough to intrigue Mrs Pretty
and to encourage her to sponsor a further programme of work the following year.

3 The great discovery, 1939

In the early summer of 1939 Brown returned to Sutton Hoo. He asked Mrs Pretty which of the remaining mounds she would like to investigate. According to his excavation diary she pointed at mound 1, the largest of the group and the one she had wanted to investigate in 1938, and said 'What about this?'. With the help once more of two of Mrs Pretty's staff – John Jacobs, a gardener, and William Spooner, her gamekeeper – Brown began as he had the previous year, by setting out a trench 6 ft wide on an east/west compass bearing through the centre of the mound. He had developed a technique in 1938 of clearing away the barrow material to the buried ground surface, and then following this towards the centre of the mound until any disturbance or break in it was encountered. He argued logically that such a disturbance would indicate a pit beneath the barrow within which he would probably find a burial. Within a couple of days of beginning the excavation the buried ground surface showed clear signs of disturbance, and the following day Jacobs, working at clearing the mound overburden, encountered an iron rivet. Thanks to his experience the previous year Brown had no problem in identifying it as a ship's rivet and his excitement began to quicken. Within a few hours of this discovery the extreme end of the ship was uncovered and Brown began to evolve a technique for emptying it of sand that was both efficient and far-sighted. He realised immediately that the wood used for building the ship had not survived and that all that was left for him to excavate was an extremely fragile impression that was formed from a thin crust of sand hardened through contact with the decaying wood that it had replaced. The rivets remained in the sand in very much their original positions so that the plank runs were instantly recognisable.

Brown's system for emptying the boat was simple: he detailed his two assistants, Spooner and Jacobs, to remove the barrow overburden and to widen the access trench into the mound while he worked inside the impression, carefully scooping out the yellow-brown sand until he came across bright orange patches which warned him that he was getting close to the iron rivets. He then, in his own words, 'crept along rivet by rivet' leaving a thin skin of undisturbed sand over the actual surface of the ship to give it some protection from sun, wind and rain, while he moved on to empty out the next stretch of the hull. It was largely because of these precautions that the hull survived from its un-covering in May until August when it was finally cleaned down for the survey and recording of the ship by the Science Museum. The volume of sand that the three men removed was enormous and as the ship plunged downwards beneath the mound and the buried ground surface, sand slips became more and more frequent until all work had to stop to widen the trench and to batter and shore its sides. Brown writes in his excavation journal of the 'terrific job' that he was facing, and as the ship grew broader and broader he began speculating on its ultimate length: 'as we go on the ship gets wider and we are certain of a length of at least 50 feet'. After a few weeks' work he realised that his ship would quite easily match and even outstrip the Oseberg and Gokstad ships and his excitement and apprehension grew together. By the time he reached the burial area amidships he had cleared a length of forty feet, the width had increased to almost fifteen feet and he had encountered the first evidence of a previous attempt to reach the burial. Ten feet below the top of the barrow lay a burnt layer – the remains of a fire – and associated with this were fragments of a Bellarmine jar dating from the late sixteenth or early seventeenth centuries. It became clear that a shaft had been sunk from the top of the mound towards the burial, which it had fortunately failed to reach, and Brown began to suspect that the burial, against all odds, had survived intact. However, he had not yet reached it, but as he was still deeply troubled by the instability of the excavation, he realised that his first priority was to make it safe by lowering the overburden of sand and widening the trench to about forty feet to reduce the danger of sand slipping back into the emptied hull. (Brown was very nearly buried by one slip of about ten tons just before he found the fragments of the Bellarmine jar.)

As it became clear to Brown that the grave was undisturbed and that he was tackling almost single-handedly a find of national, even international importance, word gradually began to leak out to the archaeological establishment that something quite extraordinary was happening in Suffolk. Although Ipswich Museum was not formally involved in the Sutton Hoo project, its curator, Guy Maynard, was a regular visitor to the site. As he watched the ship gradually emerging from its sand shroud he too became very aware that the project was developing along lines that called for a highly professional input. He contacted Charles Phillips, then a fellow of Selwyn College, Cambridge and later Archae-

10 The burial chamber, looking west, before the lifting of the objects began. The circular outlines of the bronze 'Coptic' bowl (top left), the silver Anastasius dish (centre) and the iron bands of the tub (bottom right) can just be seen.

11 The excavators studying the mass of finds beneath the Anastasius dish, with Graham Clarke (later Disney Professor of Archaeology at Cambridge) on the left, W.F. Grimes holding bellows, and Peggy and Stuart Piggott. Basil Brown stands behind them.

ological Officer to the Ordnance Survey, and invited him over to Sutton Hoo. Phillips visited the site on 6 June and was astounded at the scale of the half-excavated ship and the implications of the undisturbed burial. After his visit arrangements were quickly made to place the excavation on a more formal professional basis and Phillips was invited to take over the direction of the excavation on behalf of the Office of Works (now part of the Department of the Environment). He invited a small group of colleagues to join him – W.F. Grimes, later to become the director of the Institute of Archaeology in London, Stuart Piggott, the future Abercrombie

Professor of Archaeology at Edinburgh University, his wife (Margaret Guido), and O.G.S. Crawford, the founder and editor of the archaeological journal *Antiquity*.

Not surprisingly, it took Charles Phillips a little time to assemble his small but formidably talented team and in the intervening weeks Brown (who was to take something more of a back seat during the later phases of the excavation), after reaching the burial deposit on 15 June, was instructed to work on roughing out the western end of the great ship, but not to continue investigation of the amidships area where the burial lay. Between 19 June and 10 July

Brown, now assisted by Bert Fuller who had worked with him in 1938, removed the remaining overburden from the ship and arranged a rough protection of sacking for the eastern end. In his excavation log Brown refers to the tantalising sand-shrouded burial deposit and how the sheets of bronze that he had uncovered at the eastern end of the burial chamber 'gave out a hollow sound' when tapped.

On 10 July Charles Phillips arrived at Sutton Hoo and began working with Brown and Fuller to clear the sand lying over the burial deposit. On 19 July the Piggotts arrived and the challenging task of recording and lifting the burial deposit began. The first couple of days after the Piggotts' arrival were constantly interrupted by heavy rain which caused some sand slips. They began by defining the hump of material later called the Anastasius dish complex and carefully cleaning away the sand from the circular shape made by the great dish, thought at that time to be the remains of a shield. Next they moved to the mass of sand and wood that still covered the drinking horn group, finding traces of textiles which they left temporarily to clean a tempting area around 'a small piece of sheet iron' (in fact the tip of the sword) and almost immediately found 'a small pyramid of solid gold ... wonderfully decorated with cloisonné work and inset glass.' Despite the laconic entries in their diaries the archaeologists must have been jubilant as they uncovered remarkable finds wherever they excavated. O.G.S. Crawford, who took a series of excellent photographs of the objects in situ, joined the excavation on 24 July with W.F. Grimes, who was to take over the responsibility of lifting the deposit. Both missed by a couple of days the discovery of the sword with its gold and garnet fittings and belt mounts and two of the other most astonishing finds, the great gold buckle and the purse-lid.

But although the excavation of such an exceptionally rich grave was exhilarating, the responsibilities of recording and lifting it were heavy. Although now in the hands of archaeologists working on behalf of the Office of Works, the dig was still sponsored privately by Mrs Pretty and was in modern terms both under-financed and ill-equipped. The excavators had no proper packing materials and had to hunt around Woodbridge for grocery cartons and tobacco boxes in which to pack the finds. They collected moss from the slopes of Apricot Plantation to protect the more fragile objects and wrapped others in newspapers. Yet, despite the enormous logistical problems, the contents of the grave were lifted speedily and safely, leaving just enough time for the Science Museum to survey and record the ship's structure during August. War was declared on 3 September, only a few days after the archaeologists had packed up and left the site. In retrospect the excavation of the great ship-burial in mound 1 could be regarded as a rescue operation as Europe slid inexorably towards war and the pressures to complete the dig increased by the hour.

4 The ship

When Basil Brown began digging mound 1 he had no idea that the excavation would turn into one of the most dramatic events in British archaeology. His work in mound 2 in 1938 had prepared him for the possibility of encountering a boat and he had briefed himself by reading the accounts of the nineteenth-century discoveries of the magnificent Viking burial-ships from Gokstad and Oseberg on the Oslo fiord in Norway. He had also studied the excavation reports and finds from the Anglo-Saxon ship-burial at Snape, only nine miles away. Here in 1862 excavations had uncovered the impression of a boat about fifty feet long with rows of iron rivets almost identical in size to the ones found at Sutton Hoo. The burial had been ransacked and no traces of an amidships chamber were recorded. The few finds that had been overlooked by the grave robbers included a late antique onyx intaglio mounted in a magnificent gold filigree setting and fragments from a claw-beaker of green glass. Both these finds indicated an Anglo-Saxon grave of extremely high status, as does the form of burial in a large boat. The date of the grave is less certain as only two objects survive from it, but the latter half of the sixth century is most probable.

The Sutton Hoo ship was considerably larger than the Snape boat and its friable sandy impression survived to a length of about ninety feet. The frames, surviving only as casts, still ran sinuously across the hull from gunwale to gunwale, and the rivets remained in very much their original pos-

12 The excavated ship, looking west towards the prow. This is one of the few photographs which show the full length of the ship and the even lines of the plank fastenings running from bow to stern.

13 The after-end of the ship, showing double riveting between strake 5 and 6 port and the shadow of a thole (arrowed). In the stern are the poles and swing used by the Science Museum's team to record the rivets without standing on the ship impression.

itions so that the plank runs were as recognisable in 1939 as they were to the men who had built and buried the great ship.

After the burial deposit had been lifted the surface of the ship impression was stripped of its few protective inches of sand and work began on photographing, surveying and recording it, by a team from the Science Museum directed by Lieutenant-Commander J.K.D. Hutchison. He treated the ship impression as an archaeological project and, after the survey was complete, he cut sections across the hull to determine the structure of the keel plank and the stem and stern posts. He cleared the area where the after scarf of the keel plank and stern post survived and hunted unsuccessfully for the forward scarf. He cut a section across the prow and traced the overlapping edges of the plank ghosts as they swept up into the stem post. He cut another section outside the hull at frames 24 and 25, which were associated with the steering system, in a determined effort to discover whether there was any evidence for a large wooden boss to which the steering oar might have been attached.

At the same time that he and Charles Phillips were working to recover every small detail of the ship's structure from the sand, two holidaying schoolmistresses, Miss Mercie Lack and Miss Barbara Wagstaff, both keen amateur photographers, asked if they might join the excavations and make a photographic record of the ship. In all they took over a thousand black-and-white photographs as well as a small number of 35 mm colour transparencies and a short length of 8 mm film in which they captured the most astonishing details of the ship's original structure. It was a record that was to prove vital in the later work of reconstructing the detail of the ship as the records made by the Science Museum in August 1939 were destroyed during the war, leaving only two published, but provisional, plans that were inaccurate in many ways.

12 Although no wood survived in the ship, the impression was remarkably undistorted. This was partly because the trench that the ship lay in fitted the hull rather like a comfortable glove. Also, once 90 the burial had been laid out in the chamber amidships and roofed over, the trench would have been backfilled as the ship was packed with sand before being buried beneath its large mound. Sand is also exceptionally mobile and it will quickly fill every free space that it can, so that the hull would have been quickly encased in sand and held immobile while its planking rotted.

As the timbers decayed they were replaced by the sand and a firm skin was formed in which most of the iron rivets with the exception of those in the burial chamber were held in their original plank runs. Half-length rivets lay across the face of the strakes where two lengths of planking were joined and a stretch of double riveting remained as a graphic illustration of a repair to a sprung plank. Other areas of irregular riveting showed that two patches had been riveted to the outside of the hull, one alongside the scarf that held the keel plank to the stern post and the other amidships to port, suggesting that the ship had seen considerable service along the East Anglian coast and its estuaries. The ship was perhaps damaged as it was lowered into its burial trench, as the stern was rounded rather than sharp as the prow was. Both ends of the ship were almost certainly identical in construction, and as a rounded stern on a clinker-built hull is highly unlikely, if not impossible, it is probable that the strake ends sprang away a little from the stern post while the ship was being buried. The stress on the timbers during the tow up to the gravefield from the river would have been considerable and it is more than possible that if the ship were pushed out over rollers before being eased prow first into the trench, the stern might have been let down rather sharply as the rollers were removed.

Details of the ship's structure were preserved in two ways: firstly in the corrosion products of the ship's rivets and secondly as dark shadows in the red-brown sand. As the iron rivets corroded, the oxides migrated into the wood immediately surrounding the rivet and preserved it so that the shank of each rivet contains evidence of the thickness of the two planks that it originally fastened. On standard strake rivets the overlapping planks remain as two one-inch thicknesses of wood grain with the contact surfaces showing as a thin hard line in the middle running at right angles across the rivet shank. On the rivets that join the plank ends together, the line representing the overlap of the contact surfaces runs obliquely across the shank, showing that the ends of the planks were cut to form a simple sloping scarf. High up in the prow and stern the rivets that fastened the edges and the narrow hood ends of the planking to the stem and stern posts have an oblique line across their shanks and this reflects the contact surface of the end posts with the hoods. By measuring the distance between the contact surface of the rove end of the shank, the approximate thickness of the end post 'wings' can be gauged. Amidships, in contrast, the rivets that fasten the garboards to the keel plank display an almost horizontal contact surface and this suggests that the upper surface of the keel plank was more or less flat. The gap between the contact surface and the rove end of the shank reflects the thickness of the keel plank where it overlaps the garboard strakes.

The structure of the ship also survived as dark shadows in the sand. The most dramatic examples of this are the remains of the claw-tholes, the 13 rowlocks of the ship which were carved from naturally forked timbers (i.e. wood cut from a tree at the junction of the trunk and a branch). Each thole pin rose from an extended base and the units formed an almost continuous rail along the thickened edge of the top strake to which they were fastened by pairs, and occasionally clusters, of heavy iron spikes. The spikes show how far forward and aft the rowing positions ran, but the wood – in common with all the other wood of the ship – had decayed so that the thole-pins survived only as dark

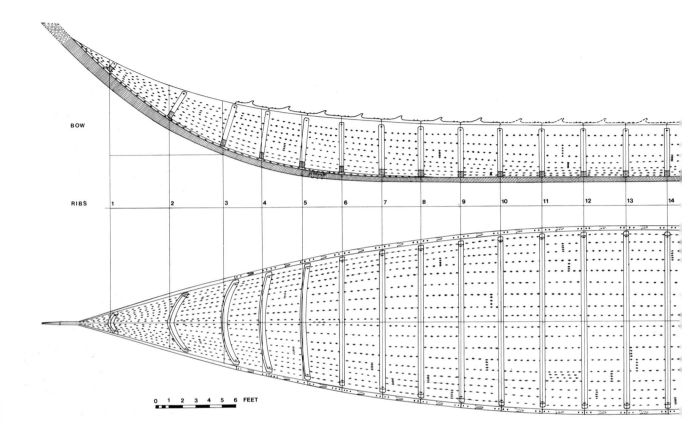

BOW

RIBS 1 2 3 4 5 6 7 8 9 10 11 12 13 14

0 1 2 3 4 5 6 FEET

14 Reconstruction of the ship based on the Science Museum's survey and the excavation photographs by Miss Mercie Lack and Miss Barbara Wagstaff. The rounded stern recorded by the Science Museum has been faired up to match the lines of the prow.

thorn-shaped shadows in the vertical face of the sand above the gunwale. Elsewhere in the ship sections cut through the keel plank at frames 8 and 9 revealed the faint outline of a stubby square keel and further forward, at frames 3, 4 and 5, the changing shadow of the stern post was revealed as it moved away from its scarf with the keel plank to develop into a deep cut-water. Hutchison also investigated the outside of the hull at frame 1 to trace the upward sweep of the planking and its relationship with the fully developed cut-water.

The hull was strengthened by twenty-six heavy frames that survived only as sand-casts running in relief across the impression of the ship. Sections cut across the frames showed that they had been trimmed square. The strake rivets that lay beneath the frames were thickly covered with decayed wood whose grain ran at right angles to the ship's planking. This must have been derived from the timber of the frames and can only have developed because the plank rivets were in direct contact with the underside of the frames while they were decaying. This implies that the underside of each frame was cut away to fit the plank overlaps so that the frames lay against the hull in much the same way as the fragmentary Gredstedbro boat – a Danish boat that is broadly contemporary with the Sutton Hoo ship. The frames were fastened to the hull by a single heavy bolt through the top strake. Elsewhere very occasional and faint circular shadows in the surface of the square-shaped casts, seen only on photographs of the excavations in 1939, suggest that trenails (wooden pegs) were used to secure the

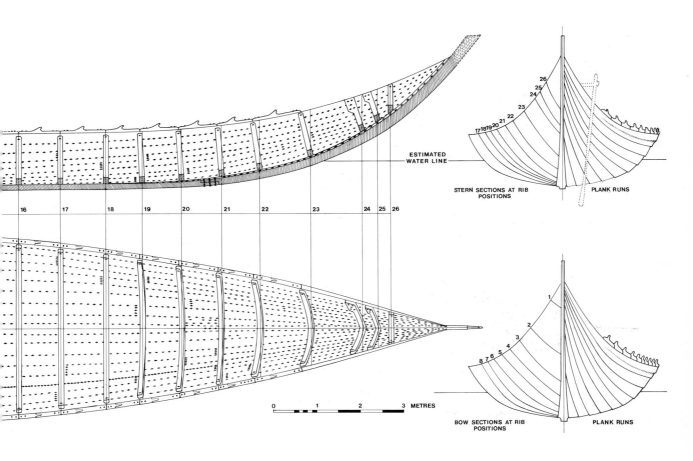

ESTIMATED
WATER LINE

STERN SECTIONS AT RIB
POSITIONS

PLANK RUNS

| 16 | 17 | 18 | 19 | 20 | 21 | 22 | 23 | 24 | 25 | 26 |

0   1   2   3 METRES

BOW SECTIONS AT RIB
POSITIONS

PLANK RUNS

frames to the planking below the top strake. High in the stern, frames 24 and 25 were closely placed and to starboard were provided with heavy expanded heads that were fastened to the hull with five and three rivets. These must have been built to take the fittings of the heavy steering oar for which no evidence survived, but it is probable that the steering system would have been dismantled before the ship was hauled uphill to her place of burial.

By piecing together tiny fragments of evidence in this way an overall picture of the ship can be built up: she was a huge open boat rowed by forty oarsmen and guided through the water by a large steering paddle that was lashed to the starboard side of the hull at frames 24 and 25. The shell of the ship was built with nine strakes to either side of a broad, flat-topped keel plank that projected stubbily into the water. Fore and aft the cut-waters projected well proud of the planking and the end posts rose

perhaps as much as 4 m above the level of the keel (their upper ends, projecting above the barrow, had been lost). Twenty-six square-cut frames strengthened the hull and these were fastened to the planking by a single iron bolt at gunwale level and wooden pegs. The ship's overall length was just over 27 m, its maximum beam 4.5 m and the depth amidships 1.5 m. No evidence survived to suggest that the ship was worked with a sail and even though a mast, if not the keelson, would almost certainly have been taken out of the ship together with the steering-oar before the portage to the grave, some evidence should have survived to indicate the use of a sail. In the excavation of the Viking-age Ladby ship, for example, four iron shroud rings survived as the only clue to the ship's use with a square sail. However the exceptional length and beamy lines of the Sutton Hoo ship may be an indication that she was more of a royal barge than a practical working ship in rather the same way as the superb ninth-century Oseberg ship. She was certainly not specially built for burial as her hull had been over-riveted and patched in several places and it is also possible that the iron bolts fastening the after scarf of the keel plank are a major repair replacing an originally trenailed scarf. She had clearly enjoyed a long working life and was perhaps only finally buried because her hull was beginning to fail.

16 ABOVE A ship from the Bayeux tapestry, showing a midships break in the rowing positions and oar-ports which were commonly used from the ninth century on larger boats.

15 Drawing by the artist Alan Sorrell showing four teams of men hauling the burial ship over rollers towards its grave.

2 The Ship Burial and its Treasures

17 The Sutton Hoo helmet. The nose and mouth, the eyebrows and the dragon head between them combine to form the image of a flying bird.

5 The burial chamber

The burial was laid out in a large chamber built in the centre of the ship between frames 9 and 16, with a length of approximately 5.5 m. Its overall width was the width of the ship, about 4.5 m, although it would have been a little less at floor level. Its height is unknown and it may have been built with a pitched roof, or planks to seal the burial could simply have been laid across the ship from gunwale to gunwale. It is clear from the 1939 excavations that the chamber had a double-skinned roof, and a solid timber framework to which the end walls were attached; no longitudinal walls existed and no details of the actual structure survived. It is also clear that the chamber was almost completely sealed from the sand that covered it and stood long enough (perhaps as long as a hundred years) not only for the helmet to corrode to a brittle state but for the ship's wood to decay and soften so that when sand eventually poured into the chamber the solid frames were flattened (in contrast to the frames outside which survived as sand casts). The ship's planking had also decayed to such an extent that the iron strake rivets had begun to slip out of their original positions, causing a slight sag in the lines of rivets which otherwise ran evenly from stem to stern where the bolts were held fast by the damp sand that filled the ship outside the chamber.

By the time that Charles Phillips arrived to take over the excavations Basil Brown had cleared the ship of almost all its filling of sand, but Phillips records that Brown had noticed 'faint signs of a possible division across the ship' on the east side of the sand-covered deposit and that similar traces, surviving only as a thin dark shadow in the sand, were found at the western end of the central area. These two faint lines running across the ship were all that remained of the once substantial end walls of the chamber. As the burial deposit was gradually uncovered dense areas of decayed wood were found lying immediately over the buried objects. The grain of the decayed wood ran along and across the deposit and must represent the collapsed internal framework of the chamber that braced the walls and supported the roof. In the south-east corner of the chamber a tiny patch of the collapsed roof survived in relatively good condition showing that it had been made of two layers of planking, the inner running across the chamber and the outer along its length.

There is little direct evidence for a floor to the burial chamber but as the frames were still in the ship when it was buried it seems probable that planking would have been placed over them to provide a flat area in the bottom of the ship on which the burial could be laid out. Supporting evidence for the existence of a floor is provided by small patches of replaced textile (textiles that survived only as impressions embedded in iron corrosion) on some of the iron objects, particularly at the eastern end of the deposit, which are the remains of a rug or mat. The spread of the floor is uncertain, but the iron bands of one of the buckets lay across the face of strakes 5 and 6 starboard and this suggests that the edge of the floor may have rested on top of strake 4, where the nearly horizontal strakes that make up the bottom of the ship begin to lift upwards into the sides of the hull.

One of the basic problems that still remains is whether the roof was pitched or flat. In 1939 Charles Phillips described the chamber as a Noah's ark construction with a pitched roof and gabled end walls. He suggested that the edge of the roof rested on the inside of the upper part of the gunwale on the basis of a short section of the starboard side of the ship between frames 12 and 13. The concept of a pitched roof was accepted by Rupert Bruce-Mitford 90 but, based on his own field experience, he interpreted the 1939 sections as representing the planks of a pitched roof running out over the top strake into the edge of the ship trench. Although a pitched roof would have given height to the chamber, it would not have effectively sealed the burial from the sandy mound that was built over the ship, whether the roof planks rested against the gunwales or ran over them, without complicated carpentry to counter the curve of the ship. There is also evidence to suggest that the very objects that needed height were in fact placed horizontally on the burial chamber floor: the stand, for example, seems to have been carefully laid parallel to the west wall and the way in which the chain was found lying in the sand suggests that it too was placed on the floor, loosely coiled near the large bronze cauldron.

An alternative system of sealing the chamber would have been a flat roof of planking running across the ship gunwale to gunwale, resting on the end walls and on the chamber's internal framework. Such a structure pre-supposes the absence of

Plate I Detail of the stag and whetstone that together make up the 'sceptre'.

rowing pins at the time of burial and this is in fact the case as there are no gunwale spikes in the burial chamber area apart from one in position at frame 10 port and a loose spike on or below the burial chamber floor near frame 10 starboard. It could be argued, of course, that the absence of rowing pins in the burial chamber is nothing to do with its structure, but is a reflection of the way in which the ship was originally designed with rowing positions forward and aft of the central area only. However, there is no evidence to suggest that the very few contemporary ships and boats did not have a continuous sweep of oars from bows to stern in contrast to some of the later Viking and Norman boats, particularly transport or cargo ships worked with sails, which may have a midships break in the rowing positions. If the midships rowing pins were removed from the Sutton Hoo ship before burial it is reasonable to assume this would have been associated with the construction of the burial chamber. But even if this is so, the evidence is so flimsy that it will not sustain a choice between a flat or a pitched roof. Both alternatives should be considered as possibilities.

The burial deposit

Within the chamber a resplendently pagan burial was set out providing the dead man with a range of possessions that reflected every aspect of his life in order to provide for his needs in the afterworld. The grave goods would have been ceremonially placed in the chamber, but such ceremony leaves no trace for future generations to find. Within the chamber there may have been a slightly raised central dais on which the principal finds were placed, for iron cleats which have no clear function in the construction of the chamber itself were found lying to either side of the central axis of the ship. Traces of textile preserved on the upper surface of some of these iron fittings suggest that the same kind of rug or mat that was used to cover the floor at the eastern end of the chamber was used in the central area as well.

The possessions that accompanied the dead man were laid out with the larger and the domestic objects against or hanging on the end walls and the more precious and personal things lying along the

Plate II A hook-escutcheon from the large hanging-bowl, with Celtic motifs reserved in red enamel and insets of brightly coloured millefiori glass.

central axis of the ship, more or less over the keel plank. Against the east wall lay a large iron-bound yew-wood tub containing a smaller bucket. Nearby were the remains of a very large cauldron of sheet bronze that had originally been hung up by one of its iron handles with its mouth against the wall. Lying in a loosely coiled heap between the cauldron and the tub, and a little way in from the chamber wall, was a corroded iron suspension chain, nearly 3.5 m long. Slightly south of the main deposit lay two small domestic objects – an iron lamp and a small pottery bottle, the only earthenware to have been placed in the burial. These rather homely objects lay alongside a piled mass of things that were covered by a large silver dish which had acted as a canopy beneath which they were reasonably protected. This large dish, called the Anastasius dish because of the silver control stamps within its foot-ring, lay immediately alongside and partially covering a deep fluted silver bowl. This had been filled with a number of small objects including a little silver bowl, a group of walnut burr-wood cups, three bone combs, one finely decorated and inlaid with an unidentifiable organic substance, and four iron knives with bone or horn handles, an otterskin cap and a wooden box mounted with four circular iron escutcheons. Alongside this bowl and beneath it was a mass of folded textiles, leather garments, the remains of four leather shoes, a group of silver and bronze buckles, a wooden scoop and a horn cup, and two bronze hanging-bowls with decorative escutcheons. On the floor of the burial beneath this mass lay a corroded shirt of mail and a curious iron axe-hammer. To the west lay a confused area containing the crushed remains of two drinking horns and a set of six maplewood drinking bottles all decorated with fragile silver-gilt mounts. The horns and bottles lay amongst the remains of piles of folded textiles.

In the space between the drinking-horn complex and the objects along the west wall of the chamber lay the possessions that would have been associated with the body of the dead man – a magnificent pattern-welded iron sword in a decayed scabbard Pl. IV and a single spear, perhaps the dead man's favourite as five others had been placed against the west wall. Gold and garnet mounts and buckles, once attached to a long decayed sword belt, lay scattered in the ground. Associated with a second belt was a stunning gold buckle, decorated all over with sinu- Pl. VII ous animal ornament, and the jewelled kidney-shaped frame and insets from the lid of a leather

33

Pl. VIII purse, long vanished, that had contained a small wealth of gold coins. At shoulder-height lay a pair
Pl. VI of magnificent gold and garnet clasps that would have fastened the two halves of a cuirass, presumably of leather as it had completely disappeared. A

little to the north-west of the shoulder-clasps were found the shattered remains of an iron helmet with Pl. III a striking face mask. Next to this lay the crushed pieces of a leather-covered limewood shield board mounted with gilt-bronze decorative devices.

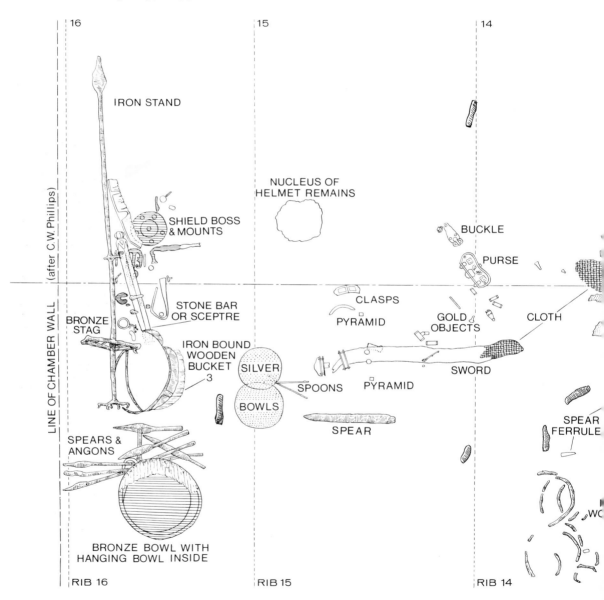

18 The layout of the burial deposit, based on Stuart Piggott's field plans and the plan published by Charles Phillips in *Antiquaries Journal* xx, 1940.

Along the west wall lay a variety of objects. In the south corner was a heavy bronze bowl made in the Coptic region of Egypt, and lying across this the burial party had placed a maplewood lyre wrapped in a beaverskin bag. On top of the lyre lay fragments of a superb Celtic hanging-bowl which had fallen Pl. II from an iron nail in the chamber wall. The shafts of three barbed throwing spears (angons) were thrust through one of the drop handles of the bronze bowl and alongside these were five iron spear heads, all

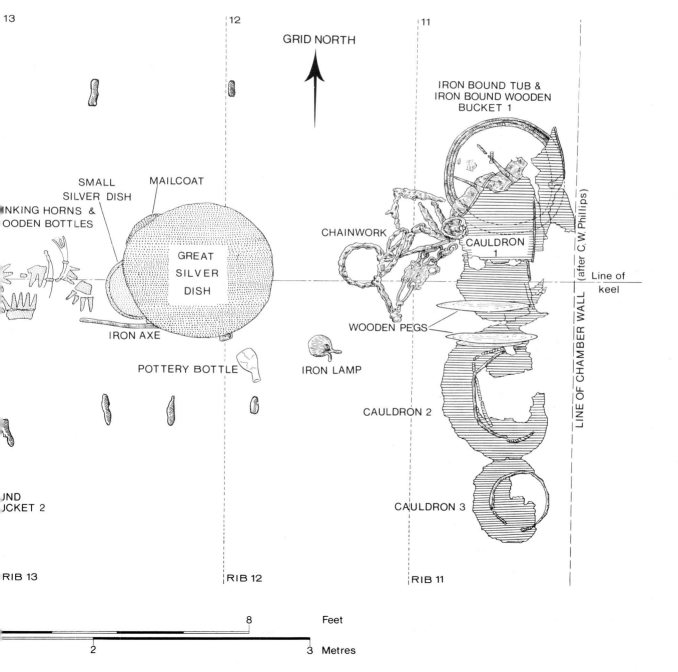

GRID NORTH

13   12   11

IRON BOUND TUB &
IRON BOUND WOODEN
BUCKET 1

SMALL
SILVER DISH

MAILCOAT

INKING HORNS &
OODEN BOTTLES

CHAINWORK

CAULDRON
1

GREAT
SILVER
DISH

(after C.W. Phillips)

Line of
keel

IRON AXE

WOODEN PEGS

POTTERY BOTTLE

IRON LAMP

CAULDRON 2

LINE OF CHAMBER WALL

UND
UCKET 2

CAULDRON 3

RIB 13   RIB 12   RIB 11

8   Feet

2   3   Metres

of different types and presumably deliberately selected from a royal arsenal. Next to the group of spears lay the iron bands of a third bucket (the second lay beyond the main burial area on the south side of the chamber) and between this and the burial chamber wall lay the upper part of an enigmatic iron object – an iron stand, over 1.5 m high – whose purpose is still not fully understood. Pl. I Lying alongside this was a massive whetstone decorated with carved faces and red painted knops.

19 The sword, showing its relationship to the shoulder-clasps and to the spoons and nest of silver bowls (above). The pommel and guards are clearly seen, as are the ring-headed strip, a rectangular mount and the strap-distributor from the sword belt (both upside down).

Loose in the sand between the whetstone and the stand the excavators found a delicately modelled bronze stag mounted on a ring of plaited iron wires. The grave goods that accompanied the dead man

20 The objects at the eastern end of the burial deposit, with Mrs Piggott working on the cauldrons and W.F. Grimes cleaning the sand from the corroded links of the chain.

on his journey to the shadowy Germanic afterlife brilliantly reflect the extraordinary variety and wealth of privileged life in the early seventh century and equally the genius of the craftsmen, probably working to commission, who created functional objects of such quality and artistic ingenuity.

The textiles

As modern archaeology recovers an increasing amount of organic material from waterlogged sites (where the lack of oxygen inhibits decay) it becomes increasingly clear that the picture archaeology provides from non-waterlogged sites can be exceptionally limited. At Sutton Hoo the acid conditions in the burial chamber had destroyed nearly every trace of wood, bone, horn, leather and cloth except

21 The edge of the mailcoat covered in replaced textiles: SH 7, a linen with wool decoration (a hanging or floor covering); SH 4, a coarse woollen weave (perhaps a blanket or a cloak) and SH 13, one of the tapes.

where they had either been protected from the hostile environment by the larger silver and bronze objects (for example the lyre inside the 'Coptic' bowl) or where, in the case of the clothing and floor coverings, they had been placed alongside iron objects. Iron can capture organic materials in its corrosion, replacing the fibres or threads with iron oxides and preserving them in almost perfect form.

In this way enough scraps of textile have survived to show that the burial chamber was once spread with fabrics of different weights and weaves.

Where the clothes had been folded and placed in piles some pieces of actual material survived in the centre of the pile, but not enough to tell us anything about their style. However, highly specialised analytical techniques have enabled archaeologists to recover something of the original gaiety of textiles, blackened by decay into unappealing scraps, by isolating traces of some of the natural dyes that were used to colour them. At Sutton Hoo, for example, the mostly woollen weaves were found to contain threads dyed with indigo or woad (SH 9), red (SH 5) and yellow (SH 10), colours that bring a new dimension to our visualisation of Anglo-Saxon life. From tiny scraps of textile it is possible to reconstruct patterned weaves (SH 14), floor coverings or wall-hangings (SH 7/5), shaggy cloaks (SH 10), fringed borders (SH 14), fine linen (SH 11 & 15), pillow/cushion coverings (SH 11 & 12), the remains of an otter-trimmed cap (SH 3), as well as many other fabrics of varying dress weights woven in tabby and a variety of twills.

Some of the weapons carry traces of the same textile (SH 8) which suggests that they may have been carefully wrapped for burial. Other iron objects, the sword and the mailcoat, preserved coiled lengths of three different tapes in their corrosion and although we do not know why these objects were buried with associated rolls of tape, or what the tapes were to be used for (unless to rebind the scabbard mouth, or secure the mailcoat), we do at least know that they were thought important enough to bury. (The roll of tape on the sword appears to have been contained in a small wooden box, whereas the coils on the mailcoat seem to have been placed loose on top of it.)

Altogether pieces of twenty-seven different textiles have been recovered from the burial. Although traces of dyes have been isolated in several of the fragments, many show no signs of having been dyed and may have been left in subtle neutral shades, just as fleece from sheep such as the Herdwick and the Jacob can produce wool which ranges in colour from pale cream to dark, almost blackish-brown, and in texture from a rough, hard-wearing yarn for weaving into close-textured heavy cloth for outdoor use to soft, finer wools for lightweight indoor clothes. The occasional seam (e.g. SH 9) shows that the standard of sewing was high and that the clothes in this royal grave were beautifully finished.

It is perhaps curious that none of the fabrics are furnished with gold thread, as was material from the Taplow burial, for example, where a fine gold wire is woven into the weft of the fabric in a variety of designs.

Although the textiles in the Sutton Hoo ship-burial survive only as dismal dark brown scraps it is possible to recreate from them an idea of the quality and wide variety of fabrics that were perhaps common amongst the upper echelons of Anglo-Saxon society.

Cenotaph or inhumation?

In 1939 the excavators had been deeply puzzled by the lack of evidence for a body in the grave. Although the personal objects lay in positions compatible with the presence of a body nothing as personal as a finger-ring, for example, had been found, and it was clear from the position of the folded piles of dress weight textiles, the four shoes and the silver and bronze buckles that they had never clothed a vanished body. No teeth were found, and no traces of bone although they were carefully looked for in the 'body' area. Out of this absence of human remains grew the theory that the ship-burial may never have contained a corpse but was instead a remarkable seventh-century cenotaph.

One alternative to the cenotaph theory was the possibility that the body had been removed soon after burial, perhaps for a Christian interment, but this does not seem to be a very realistic solution as the grave showed no signs of disturbance apart from the late sixteenth-century robbers' trench. A second alternative was the 'acid-bath' theory. It is well-known that bodies buried in acid soil will very gradually leach away leaving little evidence of their once quite substantial bulk except for a shadowy stain and the occasional tooth or fragment of dense bone. (Age also makes a difference – the bones of children and people towards the end of their life will dissolve more rapidly and completely than those of fit adults.) It was argued that in soil as generally acid as Sutton Hoo (pH 3–4) a body would disintegrate fairly rapidly after burial and that in the freak conditions of a ship-burial there would probably be a compounding of the 'acid effect'. This was because the hull would initially trap rainwater percolating from the top of the mound so that the conditions in the burial chamber would be continually damp, if not actually wet, and highly acidic. In such conditions it would not be surprising for all the organic elements in the burial to be destroyed unless they were protected to some degree through contact with corroding metals. Unfortunately, apart from the narrow iron sword blade, which was anyway sheathed in a leather-bound wooden scabbard, all the metal in the 'body' area of the burial was high quality gold which does not corrode. Thus there was no possibility of fragments of textile from the dead man's clothes being preserved, nor the leather of his shoes.

Another clue to the presence of a body would

have been given by large amounts of residual phosphates in the chamber. All living things contain phosphates and as flesh decays they are released into the surrounding environment, where they may be trapped, as for example at Sutton Hoo in the sand of the burial chamber. In 1967 the British Museum made a survey of residual phosphates throughout the burial and compared the results inside the chamber with those of the sand outside. The results showed that phosphate levels inside were markedly higher than those outside. By plotting the contours of the phosphate levels it could also be seen that the concentration increased towards the centre of the deposit where a body would have been placed. Unfortunately this process can only demonstrate that the burial chamber once contained a large phosphatic source – it cannot identify that source as being of human origin.

However, the coincidence of higher phosphate levels in the central area of the chamber must strengthen the argument that the grave is an inhumation even if it cannot entirely confirm it. This interpretation has been given additional support by the excavation of 'sand-bodies' between the 91, 92, 99 mounds and on the eastern edge of the site (chapter 12) which has demonstrated how 'bodies' can survive at Sutton Hoo in a totally decayed state in which only fragments of bone remain within a fragile concretion of sand that uncannily reflects the fleshed-out body. But in the conditions that must have existed within the chamber before the roof collapsed it is probable that the body would have decayed many years before the sand finally engulfed the burial, leaving only decayed bone to vanish into the sand. This would leave no visible trace except perhaps for a faint dark shadow in the already dark sand that fell into the chamber; it would have been a remarkable achievement for a shadow such as this to have been traced in the 1939 excavations.

6 Warrior king

The king was buried with a complete set of military equipment, designed to symbolise his warrior status and emphasise his royalty. It was placed to the east and west of the body space with the exception of the sword and a single spear which lay alongside, and the helmet which lay close to his shoulder. To the east lay a folded coat or shirt of mail and a curious long-shafted iron axe-hammer – a unique object with no immediate parallels in European archaeology. Close to the west wall was a group of five spears and three angons (barbed throwing spears) and opposite them, in the north-west corner, lay the crushed remains of a once magnificent leather-covered parade shield.

The mailcoat

The mailcoat and axe-hammer were buried with the dead man's personal possessions. The mailcoat, folded several times, was placed on the burial chamber floor across the axis of the ship. A leather garment or skin was spread over it and the fluted silver bowl was placed on top, its foot-ring pressing through the leather into the supple links.

The mail had corroded into a solid mass of iron rings so dense that radiography was unable to recover any details but its bulk suggests that it may have been at least thigh-length. It was made of finely forged iron links a uniform 8 mm in diameter with rows alternately butt-jointed and riveted with tiny copper rivets. When worn the mail would have been heavy but supple and strong, capable of protecting against spear and sword thrusts.

No similar mass of mail has yet been found in a contemporary European context although the technique of manufacture was known as fragments are occasionally found in high-status graves. Face and neckguards of mail of similar manufacture are also known from the chieftains' graves of Vendel and Valsgärde in Sweden and from the slightly later helmet from Coppergate, York.

The axe-hammer

The axe-hammer is made entirely of iron and consists of an axe-like head forged onto a long iron shaft. It lay touching the folded mail, to which it had corroded. The weapon has a blunt hammer-like extension to the head which is only paralleled on certain types of tool, for example the blacksmith's sett or the wooden-hafted axe-hammer heads that are occasionally excavated. The exceptionally long iron shaft ends in a rounded element to which a small iron ring was attached. Radiographs have identified this as a swivelling device, and it is probable that the iron ring would have held a carrying-strap in much the same way as a modern knob-kerry. Although the axe-hammer has no direct parallels, its association with the mailcoat, together with its large size (78 cm overall) and iron construc-

22 One of the smaller fragments of the mailcoat, showing rows of links and individual links at the edge.

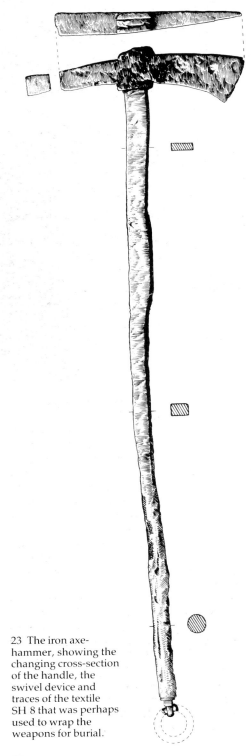

tion suggests that it was a weapon rather than a tool. Its nearest parallel may lie in a medieval context as part of the equipment of the mounted soldier, although there is no evidence for such specialised equipment in Anglo-Saxon England. Alternatively it may be a two-handed fighting axe similar to those shown in the Bayeux tapestry.

The spears and angons

The dead man's weapons included five spears and three angons that were found corroded together in the south-west corner of the chamber and a single spear alongside the sword. The angons had been pushed through one of the heavy drop handles of the 'Coptic' bowl so that their long iron necks were trapped in the handle. The five spears lay in an untidy heap with one lying beneath the 'Coptic' bowl, suggesting that it may perhaps have been placed on a low shelf. The sixth spear, deliberately set apart from the main group, and placed parallel with the sword, may well have been the dead man's most treasured one. The spears fall into two main groups with either leaf-shaped or straight-sided blades but each one is quite different from the others and the complex gives the impression of careful selection for burial.

Spears are one of the most common objects found in Anglo-Saxon graves but only a few graves contain more than two (Garton in Yorkshire, for example, contained seven and Hardown Hill, Wiltshire, six). Sutton Hoo is unique in containing a group of six different types of spear as well as three angons.

The sword

The magnificent pattern-welded sword lay beside its owner. Its suspension belt lay alongside and even partially underneath as its gold and garnet buckle was found crushed by the blade. The sword was buried in a scabbard that was made of wood and lined with wool chosen for its oily texture to keep the costly blade bright. Its mouth was tightly bound for over 16 cm with overlapping turns of a fine, narrow tape (SH 16) and two coils of the same tape lay beneath the scabbard.

The blade is made from eight bundles of iron rods hammered together to form a patterned core to which the cutting edge of high carbon steel was forged. Radiography shows that four bundles of seven thin iron rods were twisted alternately to the

23 The iron axe-hammer, showing the changing cross-section of the handle, the swivel device and traces of the textile SH 8 that was perhaps used to wrap the weapons for burial.

24 The 'Coptic' bowl, with the long iron necks of the three angons (throwing spears) thrust through one of its drop handles. Three of the spears lie alongside, together with the socket of a fourth, whose head lies behind the bowl. The fifth spear has been lifted by the excavators.

right and left to create a herringbone pattern or left untwisted to create a pattern of parallel lines. They were then laid back to back with four more bundles of seven rods so that the plain and herringbone patterns on each face alternate. Two long strips of iron were forged to this complex central core to form the cutting edge and at the top the blade develops a small, narrow tang enclosed in a wooden grip.

Pattern-welded sword blades were amongst the most highly prized possessions and were often handed down from generation to generation and even named. The Sutton Hoo sword is one of the finest to have survived and it is not surprising that both it and the scabbard should have been mounted Pl. IV with superb gold and cloisonné garnet fittings. The hilt has a gold and cloisonné garnet 'cocked-hat' pommel and upper and lower guards of sheet gold.

Between the guards was a wooden handgrip decorated with two delicate gold filigree clips. The pommel is made up of five separate units of exquisite workmanship – two convex side panels, two narrow concave upper panels and a small square unit forming the top. These were placed edge to edge around a bronze former to which they were nailed and the deep angles between them were filled with thick beaded gold wire. The upper and lower guards are made of sheets of gold wrapped around a decayed metallic core. They are roughly pierced for the tang, and thick gold rope collars that originally bound the hand-grip remain soldered to them.

On the scabbard lay two robust gold and garnet fittings in the shape of domed buttons or bosses. Each is decorated with a geometrically precise petalled design that contains within it a subtle equal armed cross whose cells are filled with red garnets that are lighter in colour than the more purple garnets in the fields between the arms. Two rows of relief cut garnets form a border to this intricate design. The ability to select garnets of different colour implies that the jeweller had a variety of stones to select from.

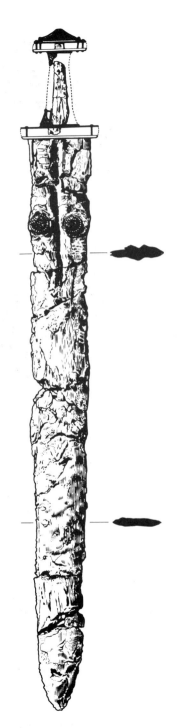

Each boss has a long staple soldered to the back-plate and this originally pierced a heavy collar of bone or ivory, raising the boss above the surface of the scabbard. The function of the bosses is not clear as their staples apparently did not pierce the scabbard itself. They may have been attached to the upper of two leather loops that encircled the scabbard as part of the two-point suspension harness that secured the sword to the sword-belt.

In the sand to either side of the sword and level with the scabbard bosses lay a small pyramid-shaped mount. Made of gold and set with cloisonné garnets with a single millefiori inset, these little mounts together with the scabbard bosses are in Bruce-Mitford's words perhaps 'the most astonishing examples of technical virtuosity seen in the Sutton Hoo jewellery'. The pyramids are strongly made and hollow in construction with a bar across the open base that creates two slots through which a thin leather strap could have been threaded. Each face of the pyramids shares a common design with a central panel of cloisonné garnets enclosed by a thick wall of gold. The edges of the pyramids are made from precisely cut and faceted garnets, separated by narrow bands of dark blue glass, that are set directly on the bottom of the cell so that in oblique light the highly polished gold shines clearly through the garnet. A piece of blue and white chequer-board millefiori glass is set into the top of each pyramid. The function of the pyramids is not entirely clear, but their position in the ground, together with their practical design and the evidence of similar pyramidal mounts, suggests that they were threaded with narrow straps and used to adjust the sword harness, perhaps the tension of the loop which gripped the upper part of the scabbard.

Lying towards the bottom of the sword blade and a little to the north of it was a curved slider in the form of a narrow, triangular dummy buckle made in gold and decorated with cloisonné and cabochon garnets. The face of the slider is dominated by three bosses that disguise the heavy gold rivets that originally secured it to a strap looped around the scabbard. Two of these contain cabochon garnets while the third, forming the toe of the slider, contains a raised cloisonné setting of five garnets.

The curve of the slider matches that of the scabbard and originally it would have held the end of a strap that fell from the distributor on the sword belt. The end of this strap would have been fed through the slider's garnet-mounted loop before running under the scabbard and curving round to lie between the slider and its thin backplate where it

25 The sword. The drawing shows the wooden hilt reconstructed and mounted with two filigree clips.

was securely fixed by the three rivets. The whole unit acted as a supplementary suspension point for the lower part of the sword.

The sword belt

Although the sword lay in the ground with its jewelled pommel level with the shoulder-clasps, the fittings of the scabbard and sword belt suggest that it was worn at the waist slung from a heavy leather belt and steadied by a strap that fell from the waist belt to the scabbard. No trace of the belt survived apart from its gold and garnet fittings, which were probably made as a set in the same workshop, as their structural details are nearly identical. Each piece has a decorative display surface set with intricate and beautifully executed designs in cloisonné garnet. They have flat shoulders decorated with garnets and pierced by three-dome headed gold rivets with filigree collars. The rivets were clenched over gold backing plates on the inside of the belt. The gap between the mounts and their backplates is 2 mm, the thickness of the belt to which they were attached. The width of the belt is

26 Gold and garnet fittings from the scabbard and the sword belt: (top) the scabbard slider, strap-distributor and rectangular buckle; four rectangular mounts, two with cable-twist decoration (left) and two with an overall pattern of stepped mushroom cells (right).

more difficult to calculate, but it must have been at least 20 mm, the width of the mounts, which would give a narrow, but quite substantial belt. It was fastened by a rectangular buckle found crushed beneath the sword and the only piece of jewellery in the burial to have been damaged. Its panelled surface is filled with an intricate and repeating design in finely executed cloisonné garnets. It was attached to the waist-belt by five gold rivets that were clenched over a strong backplate.

Close to the sword, face down in the sand lay a gold and garnet strap-distributor. It would originally have been mounted on the belt almost immediately above the hip, conveniently placed for a strap to drop to the scabbard slider. The distributor is made up of three elements. A rectangular mount decorated with a beautifully balanced geometric design in cloisonné garnet work was attached to the waist-belt. Soldered to its lower edge is a hinge whose semi-circular barrels are decorated with a design based on honeycomb cells. The hinge holds a garnet-set element with a semi-circular terminal on which a tightly fitting strap-holder pivots and from this a strap 14 mm wide and 2 mm thick ran to the gold and garnet scabbard slider. The distributor was in perfect working order when it was excavated – the hinged element can move backwards and forwards through 110 degrees and the swivelling strap-end moves from side to side through an arc of 40 degrees. It is one of the burial's more remarkable objects and displays the same mechanical ingenuity combined with a superbly balanced design as the gold buckle that fastened the purse belt.

Between the sword and the purse-lid lay four rectangular strap-mounts belonging to the sword belt. From their positions in the ground their distribution on the belt can be reconstructed: one was mounted between the rectangular buckle and the strap-distributor, while the other three would have been equally spaced between the strap-distributor and the belt's tongue. They are designed as matching pairs, one decorated with interlocking mushroom cells, the other filled with an overall geometric design of eight step-patterned cells enclosed within cable-twist borders.

The sword-belt fittings display the same sure quality of workmanship as the shoulder-clasps and the purse-lid although in a sense they are minor objects in comparison. They show no signs of repair and very little wear, which suggests either that they were relatively new when they were placed in the grave or that the sword and its belt had rarely been worn – perhaps only used on ceremonial occasions as would befit such costly yet functional mounts.

The helmet

Perhaps the most immediately spectacular finds in the Sutton Hoo ship-burial are the magnificent helmet and shield that lay crushed by the timbers of the collapsed burial chamber and smothered by the sand that engulfed them. The iron helmet lay broadly level with the dead man's head and a little to the north of it. In the collapse the iron had shattered into tiny pieces but because it had corroded in an open space it was undistorted and so it has been possible at least to restore the helmet to its original shape.

Like the chainwork, the helmet is a remarkable example of the metalsmith's skill: the cap is forged from a single piece of iron and to it were attached

deep iron ear-flaps and a broad and equally deep iron neckguard. The surface of the iron was covered with sheets of tinned-bronze foil which would have given the helmet a silvery appearance that can be seen now only on the replica. The plates were held by fluted bronze strips that divide the helmet into clearly defined zones and the edges of the cap, ear-flaps and neckguard were bound with channelled bronze strips. These enclosed the iron and the edges of the tinned-bronze plates and were held in place by nails and fluted bronze clips.

The tinned-bronze plates were stamped with four different decorative motifs. Two are of sinuous animal interlace and two are filled with figural 28, 29 scenes from Germanic and Scandinavian mythology. One of these is a beautifully designed scene showing a mounted warrior riding down a fallen mail-clad warrior who stabs the horse as it rides over him. This scene has its roots in the Roman period and is found in various guises within northern Europe and Scandinavia but the origins of the other scene showing dancing warriors is obscure. Its distribution however lies in eastern England and Sweden and suggests that it belongs within Scandinavian mythology.

The helmet has a low crest of iron inlaid with Pl. III silver wire with gilt-bronze terminals in the form of stylised animal heads with cabochon garnet eyes, open jaws and gnashing teeth. Two cast bronze eyebrows are attached to the front of the cap. These are inlaid with silver wire and decorated with small square-cut garnets that are set in individual bronze cells. The eyebrows have gilt-bronze terminals in the form of a boar's head. The helmet has an oval iron face mask to which is attached a realistically modelled nose and mouth made of thickly gilded and lavishly decorated cast bronze. The nose is cast in high relief and is hollow with two nostril-holes immediately above the toothbrush moustache. Behind the nose casting the iron of the face mask is cut away for the wearer's nose. The face mask is covered with large sheets of tinned-bronze foil stamped with impressions of the narrow panel of animal interlace. It is fixed rigidly to the helmet cap in contrast to the ear-flaps and neckguard which hung freely from the cap on leather hinges attached

27 Replica of the helmet in steel, made by the armourers of the Tower of London, with electrotype panels and strips. The replica shows how the surface of the helmet is divided into decorative zones and recreates the silvery appearance of the original.

28 TOP The fallen warrior scene from the helmet, built up from tiny areas of the design that survived on the helmet's surface. Gaps in the design are shown in dotted line.

29 Reconstruction of the dancing warrior scene from the helmet. In such scenes on both Swedish and English metalwork the warriors' helmets are crowned with bird-headed horns.

Plate III The Sutton Hoo helmet.

Plate IV The gold and garnet fittings from the sword: (top) the 'cocked-hat' pommel; (centre) the lower guard showing the filigree rope that was wrapped around the hand-grip, and the two scabbard bosses; (bottom) the filigree clips from the grip, flanked by the pyramids that dangled on thin leather straps to either side of the scabbard.

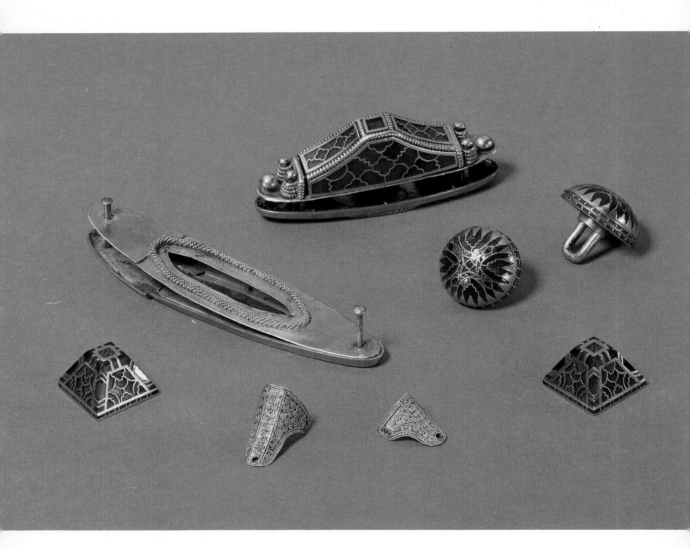

to the iron by small plates riveted through the metal. The front edges of the ear-flaps are curved to match the face mask so that when they are pulled towards the face and tied beneath the chin, the face is completely protected. Inside, the helmet is covered with a glassy corrosion. This is unlike the usual bubbling corrosion found on other iron objects in the burial and is thought to be a corroded leather lining. It may have been padded to make the helmet more comfortable to wear. The replica helmet, made by the Tower of London Armouries, is lined with chamois leather to illustrate this.

The Sutton Hoo helmet has it roots in the parade helmets of the late Roman Empire but its immediate ancestry lies in a group of helmets buried in the 96 chieftains' graves of Vendel and Valsgärde in the Uppland region of Sweden, just north of Stockholm. Here, in the sixth, seventh and eighth centuries the chief families of the region buried their dead in ships beneath low circular mounds accompanied by all the wealth they enjoyed during their lifetime. The helmets that lay with the dead are magnificent and are superficially remarkably similar to the Sutton Hoo helmet. But there are significant differences, particularly in the way that they were made, that suggest that the Sutton Hoo helmet is English rather than Swedish. The most important difference is that the cap of the Sutton Hoo helmet is forged from a single sheet of iron, whereas the Swedish helmets are either made in sections or of iron strips. The Swedish helmets do not have solid iron face-masks, ear-flaps and neckguards but use instead a system of bronze visors, mail curtains and narrow iron strips. It is only in its surface decoration that the Sutton Hoo helmet clearly displays its Swedish ancestry and it is possible that the helmet plates were made by Swedish craftsmen working at the East Anglian court or that dies made in Scandinavia were used. The discovery in York in 1983 of a magnificent iron helmet dating from the late seventh or early eighth century provides an English context for the unusual features of the Sutton Hoo helmet – especially the deep ear-flaps and solid cap – and although there are only two helmets of this structure known, they may represent an English tradition that developed independently from the Roman parade helmets.

The shield

The shield lay on the burial chamber floor immediately to the west of the helmet and survived only as a jumbled group of metal fittings associated with 30 tiny scraps of the limewood and leather that once formed its massive board. It has been reconstructed with a diameter of 91.5 cm – the minimum size that will comfortably accommodate all the mounts – with a board shaped rather like a giant watchglass. The 31 shield was made of limewood and covered with hide which was probably glued to the board although no trace of any adhesive survived. The rim was bound by a gilt-bronze strip, clamped to the board and held in position by a series of gilt-bronze clips. Associated with these are pairs of gilt-bronze dragon heads with garnet eyes that flank rectangular panels of gilt-bronze foil decorated with animal interlace.

At the centre of the board is a magnificent and highly decorated iron boss with a cast bronze knop 32 decorated with a frieze of animals, each with a garnet eye, surrounding a cloisonné garnet disc. The Sutton Hoo boss is remarkably similar to some of the shield bosses from the high-status graves of Vendel and Valsgärde in Sweden, particularly 95 Vendel XII, shield 1, and if it was not actually made in Sweden it was certainly made by Swedish armourers.

To either side of the boss lie two remarkable shield mounts – one an exquisitely designed dragon 34 cast in bronze, the other a bird of prey seen in 35 profile whose head and leg are cast in bronze, but whose body, wing and tail were made from gold foil. The dragon is a unique creation, a long distant relative of openwork iron dragons that occasionally decorate Swedish shields, but the bird of prey belongs to a vast family of similar hunting bird mounts, fittings and brooches that are found frequently throughout northern Europe and Scandinavia.

Above and below the boss are a series of high-domed gilt-bronze bosses with tinned collars which disguise rivets that hold the fittings on the back of the shield to the board. Two are placed above and below the boss and from them gold foil strips wrapped around alderwood underlays extend across the face of the shield. The foil is impressed with a design of animal interlace that is almost indistinguishable from interlace decorating strips on a shield from Vendel grave XII, and the Sutton Hoo strips may have been made in the same workshop or by the same Swedish metalsmith. The gold foil strips are a decorative echo of functional strips, often of iron, that held the boards of fighting shields together, and this, combined with the fragility and

30 The metal fittings of the shield: the photograph shows one of the hand-grip extensions, the gilt-bronze dragon and the boss. At this end of the burial the chamber wall was forced inwards, pushing the fittings of the decayed shield board towards the boss.

wealth of the other mounts, suggests that the Sutton Hoo shield was intended for formal display and not necessarily for combat.

A gilt-bronze 'ring' was mounted at the bottom of the shield. The 'ring' was lifted in a mass of shield fragments and was not found until the remains were examined in the British Museum Research Laboratory after the end of the Second World War.

It was not at first realised that the 'ring' had come from the shield as it belongs to a group of objects that are normally attached to sword pommels, but a small piece of the shield board was found that was impressed with the outline of the 'ring' and this showed that it had originally been part of the shield. Fragments of alderwood with flakes of gold foil were found with the piece of shield board and it was realised that the 'ring' had been set on a foil-covered strip on the front of the shield. The only other 'ring' apart from Sutton Hoo that is not associated with a sword is from one of the ship-burials in the Valsgärde cemetery (no. 7) where a similar 'ring' was

36

31 Front view of the
reconstructed shield: the board is
modern and made from
limewood covered with oak-bark
tanned hide; the rim fittings, the
strips, the collars of the four
small bosses and the body of the
bird are all electrotypes.

32 The shield boss: the flange
and neck are decorated with
panels of gilt-bronze foil held by
fluted strips and clips that were
riveted through the iron. On the
dome the gilt-bronze animal
heads are shaped over beeswax
so that they stand out in relief.

33 ABOVE One of the panels of gilt-bronze foil from the flange of the shield boss, impressed with a design of four interlaced horses.

34 Gilt-bronze dragon with a cabochon garnet eye and gnashing teeth. Flat circular garnets lie at the centres of the twists from which the folded wings and tail develop.

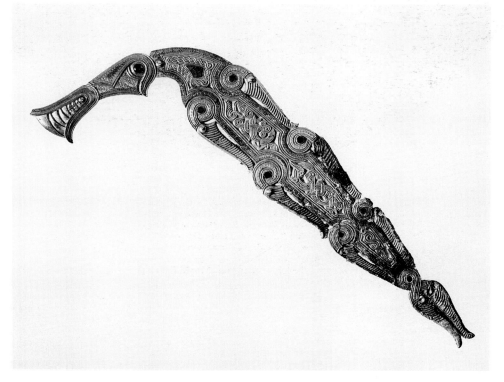

35 LEFT The bird of prey, whose body, wing and tail were originally made of gold foil impressed with animal interlace and mounted on alderwood. The gilt-bronze head and leg are decorated with cloisonné garnets and superbly executed punch-work. The bird's foot is tinned and the talons gilded.

36 Gilt-bronze 'ring' that was originally mounted on the front of the shield at the centre of an alderwood strip covered with gold foil.

37 One of the ornamental hand-grip extensions from the back of the shield, made partly of iron wrapped in gold foil and partly of gilt-bronze decorated with tinning and finely executed punch-work.

found mounted on a strip on a drinking horn. The symbolism behind these 'rings' is not clearly understood. References in Anglo-Saxon poetry describe the king as the 'giver of rings' but do not define what kind of rings are meant. Some at least were associated with deeds of valour and were perhaps akin to modern concepts of awards for bravery.

The shield was held by an iron hand-grip with ornate foil-covered extensions. It was placed off-centre across a hole cut in the back of the board behind the central boss. Above the hand-grip extensions are a pair of fittings that may have been used to carry the shield and to hang it up. At the top of the shield is a pair of tinned-bronze plates joined by a U-shaped link which holds a fitting that is also made of tinned bronze. This contains a fragment of leather, perhaps the end of a narrow carrying strap used to sling the shield across the back. Below this is a thick tooled leather strap with tinned-bronze strap-ends that may have been used to hang the shield up when it was not being carried.

The shield has frequently been described as Swedish, although the extraordinary quality of its fittings is not paralleled in Swedish contexts. Despite this, the magnificent iron boss, the foil strips and the designs used to decorate the dragon can only have been created by craftsmen who had worked in the milieu that produced the Vendel XII shields. The richness of the Sutton Hoo shield with its limewood construction may suggest that it was assembled by Swedish craftsmen working to commission in the workshops of the royal Anglian court.

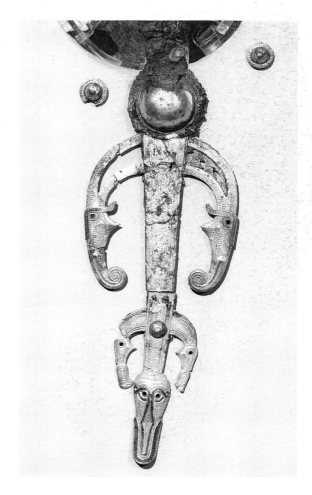

38 The Anastasius dish.

39 Impressions of two control stamps from inside the foot-ring of the Anastasius dish. The stamps date the dish to the reign of the Emperor Anastasius I (AD 491–518).

7 Mediterranean silver

Apart from the gold and garnet jewellery the most impressive symbol of wealth in the Sutton Hoo ship-burial is the lavish provision of silver to accompany the dead man. Sixteen pieces were placed in the grave in two distinct groups, one near his right shoulder at the west end of the burial, the other on the central axis of the deposit beyond the drinking horn complex.

The silver in the Sutton Hoo burial is the largest collection yet found in a purely archaeological context, although equal or larger quantities have been found in hoards. It was probably all made in east Mediterranean workshops and presumably reached north-west Europe along the riverine trading routes. It may well have found its way into East Anglia via Merovingian Gaul as a diplomatic gift.

The Anastasius dish and fluted bowl

The largest of the sixteen pieces is the Anastasius dish with a diameter of 72.4 cm. Made from a single lump of silver, it is essentially a broad platter with an abnormally deep foot-ring. The dish is decorated with zones of small-scale incised ornament based on geometric and floral designs. In the centre is a roundel containing an eight-pointed star and set within this is a bird, probably an eagle. Between the rim and the central zone of decoration is a narrow band of ornament separated by four roundels. Two of these contain seated figures, perhaps representing Rome and Constantinople, the twin capitals of the Empire, and two contain running figures with flowing drapery.

The foot-ring is remarkably deep and is stamped on the inside with impressions of two control stamps of the Emperor Anastasius I (AD 491–518) which make it clear that the dish was an antique at the time of its burial. It is an object with no direct parallels although other large and splendid dishes are well-known from this period. None of them share the small-scale, rather fussy, decoration of the Anastasius dish, and none have a similar style of foot-ring. This, and the careless way in which the decoration was applied to its surface, suggests that the dish does not come from one of the key workshops in the Byzantine Empire, but is the product of a second-rate artisan who nonetheless produced a piece of silver that is visually impressive even if it is not a work of high artistic quality.

The fluted bowl also suffers from careless execu- 41 tion which suggests that it too is the product of a second-rate workshop, but its overall effect is pleasing. The bowl stands on a small foot-ring and is 40 cm in diameter with a flat out-turned rim with a beaded edge. Its body is hammered up into narrow flutes and at the centre within a double border is the head of a woman with piled hair and wearing a diadem. The head is awkwardly placed within the roundel so that the luxuriant hair touches the border, throwing the design off balance. Another curious feature is the unfilled depression made by the lathe chuck which disfigures the jaw.

When the bowl was lifted a clear impression of its fluted outline could be seen in the leather that lay between it and the mailcoat. To either side of its impression lay two pairs of circular silver escutcheons supporting silver drop handles. At first these were thought by the excavators to belong to a leather bag, but scars on the outside of the fluted bowl showed that the handles were once soldered to it.

The fluted bowl contained among a mass of other things (page 33) a small silver cup (diameter 8 cm) 42 with a shallow curved body and a plain out-turned lip, disfigured by two small holes that may have held the rivets of a small repair patch. The cup sits on a heavy foot-ring to which it was once soldered.

A parcel-gilt ladle was placed amongst the textiles outside the fluted silver bowl and immediately beneath the Anastasius dish so that the dish's foot-ring pressed down onto it and its bowl became 40 pinched on to the rim of the foot-ring. The bowl has a sharply angular profile and is decorated at the rim 43 and carination with lightly incised triangles with gilded fields. The ladle has a robust handle that ends in a loop through which is threaded a loose ring of heavy silver wire.

40 The Anastasius dish immediately after it had been lifted, with the ladle bowl still pinched onto its deep foot-ring.

41 The rather battered fluted bowl with the drop handles that were originally soldered to it. The bowl was crushed against the mailcoat, which rusted around it so that the bowl's outline survives in the corroded links.

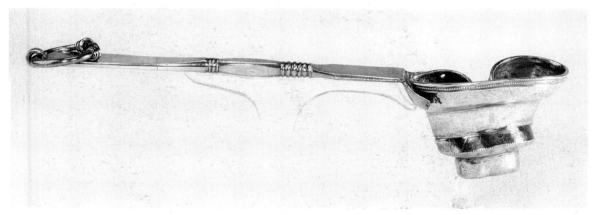

Nest of bowls and two spoons

42 TOP The small silver cup and the bowl of the ladle
damaged by the foot-ring of the Anastasius dish. The
finely incised outlines of the lower frieze of gilded
triangles on the ladle are just visible.

43 The silver ladle, showing the decorative scheme
of beading and gilded triangles and details of the strong
baluster handle.

At the other end of the central deposit lay the ten
silver bowls and two spoons. Their placing, near the
dead man's shoulder, suggests a more personal
significance than the silver in the Anastasius dish
complex and because each bowl is decorated with
an equal-armed cross and the spoons are inscribed
in Greek 'Saulos' and 'Paulos', a Christian significance has in the past been attached to the group.
However, while the names 'Saulos' and 'Paulos'
must have an ultimately Christian significance,
there is nothing in the decoration of the bowls to

suggest that they have a Christian connotation. Very similar shallow silver bowls, but with overtly Christian crosses, are found in other collections of silver, for example the Lampsacus treasure in the British Museum that also contains the closest parallels to the Sutton Hoo spoons.

Eight bowls survive in excellent condition because of the way they were stacked one inside the other and inverted so that nearly all of them were protected from the destructive effect of the acidic sand that covered them when the chamber roof fell in. All the bowls have a gently curving profile that is uninterrupted by a foot-ring, which makes them inherently unstable. Each bowl is decorated with a similar device of an equal-armed cross springing from a central roundel but the decorative details vary so that the bowls can be loosely divided into

44 One of the ten shallow silver bowls that were piled one inside the other, preventing corrosion. The bowl is repaired with a gilt stud that forms the eye of the central flower.

pairs. The designs are all incised and in some cases are textured with punches to provide a greater contrast with the highly polished areas of the bowls. Manufacturing repairs can be seen on two of the bowls: one has been repaired with a dome-headed gilt stud that forms the centre of a multi-petalled flower and another bowl has a small silver patch over a tear in the rim.

Alongside the bowls lay two spoons of a well-known late classical type. These are a mould pair and are identical in all ways except for the names that are inscribed in Greek on their handles. They have pear-shaped bowls that are attached to long

46

45 A second silver bowl with a large central flower whose petals show how texturing tools were used to roughen the surface of the silver to contrast with the highly polished areas.

moulded handles by a plain and vertically set disc. The inscriptions on their handles have provoked a mass of conflicting interpretation. One clearly reads 'Paulos' in a well organised inscription competently executed with a half-circular punch. The other, executed by a different hand in a similar but careless manner, reads 'Saulos'. On the strength of the inscriptions, the spoons have been interpreted as a direct Christian statement referring to the conversion of St Paul on the road to Damascus. This Christian link has been used as an indication that the man buried in the grave is Raedwald, king of the East Angles (d. 624/5), who was briefly converted to Christianity but soon reverted to paganism and subsequently maintained altars to his pagan deities alongside a Christian altar (see chapter 13).

It has also been argued that the Saulos inscription is an illiterate attempt to copy the name Paulos, suggesting that both spoons are intended to read Paulos, weakening the reference to St Paul's conversion. It has moreover been pointed out that the technique used to cut the inscriptions is the same as that used to cut inscriptions on coins, where mistakes sometimes occur in joining up the gouged-out points of each letter. This could well have happened on the initial S of the Saulos spoon. However, even if the spoons were originally inscribed as a deliberately Christian statement, it should perhaps be asked whether in an East Anglia that was only on the very brink of conversion in the early seventh

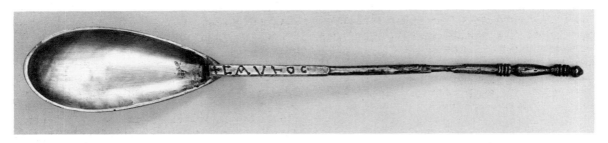

46 The pair of silver spoons inscribed in the Greek alphabet with the names of Saul and Paul.

47 Heavy bronze 'Coptic' bowl from the east Mediterranean.

century, there was anyone, priest or king, who could interpret the Greek lettering on the spoons or whether the spoons had come into East Anglia, perhaps with the rest of the silver, simply as a gift and that their inscriptions were of no great consequence to the people who ultimately buried them. Their significance as a possible symbol of Christianity should not be overstated.

The 'Coptic' bowl

The sixteen pieces of silver are not the only objects manufactured in the eastern Mediterranean to have found their way into the Sutton Hoo ship-burial. In the north-west corner of the chamber was a large bronze bowl which contained a large hanging-bowl and the remains of a musical instrument.

The bowl is large and heavy with a flat out-turned rim and rounded body set on a sturdy foot-ring. Two heavy drop handles are attached to lugs cast into the body. Inside, the bowl is finished with shallow flutes that enclose a frieze of rather ineptly drawn marching animals. Inside the bowl is finished with shallow flutes that enclose a frieze of rather carelessly drawn animals. Three can probably be identified as a bear, a lion and a hare, while the fourth could be either a hound or a second feline.

The 'Coptic' bowl belongs to a well-defined group of bronzes from the east Mediterranean and over twenty have been found in Anglo-Saxon contexts. They are characterised by their distinctive range of shapes – bowls, jugs, censers and tripod jars – and are cast in a copper alloy containing a high percentage of zinc. They are popularly known as 'Coptic' because of an apparent concentration of workshops in the Coptic areas of Egypt around the Nile delta and Alexandria, but modern research now suggests that the workshops producing such bronzes were more widely spread around the eastern Mediterranean and that the use of the word 'Coptic' to describe them is misleading.

The immediate area of Sutton Hoo has also produced a bucket from an east Mediterranean workshop. This is of raised copper-alloy and is decorated with a hunting frieze beneath a dedicatory inscription. This bucket, a stray find from a field a kilometre north of the cemetery, belongs to a small group of similar buckets with find spots as far apart as Turkey, the Isle of Wight and Spain. They are thought to have been manufactured in military workshops in Antioch or Constantinople. The bucket, like the cast bronze bowl from the ship-burial, is another indication of the widely spread contacts of the East Anglian kingdom in the early seventh century.

48 Procession of animals engraved on the inside of the 'Coptic' bowl.

8 Feasting in the great hall

The drinking horns and maplewood bottles

At the dead man's feet the burial party placed piles of folded clothes and on these laid two magnificent drinking horns and a set of maplewood bottles all decorated with silver-gilt fittings. When the excavators uncovered the drinking-horn complex in 1939 they were confronted with a compressed mass of decayed textile and wood in which the pale purplish outlines of the silver-gilt foils that originally decorated the horns and bottles could be seen. Rather than investigate the fragile complex during the excavations it was decided to lift it in sections for excavation in controlled laboratory surroundings. The salvaging of the fragile mounts and the fragments of wood and horn was accomplished

with a delicacy and sureness of touch that led to the successful reconstruction of the horns and bottles (see chapter 11).

The pair of drinking horns were recognised from the remains of their terminals, which lay almost touching each other in the ground, and their silver-gilt mouth fittings. The horns had been placed among the textiles so that their ends overlapped and their curving bodies encircled all but one of the maplewood bottles. Although all the horn had vanished with the exception of one tip, the four rectangular panels that were mounted around each rim show that the horns had a mouth diameter of

49 Artist's impression of how the drinking horns and maplewood bottles may have been placed in the burial chamber.

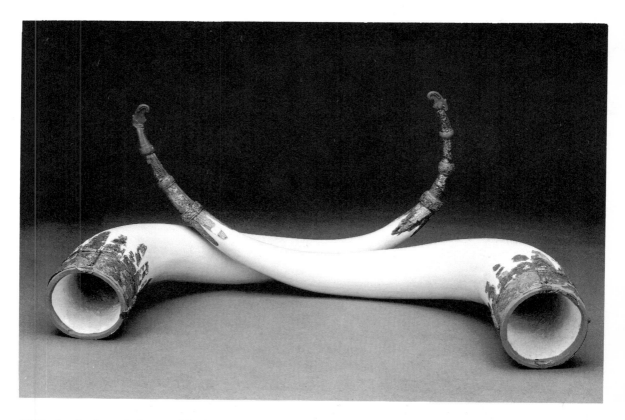

50 The fragile silver-gilt fittings of the drinking horns mounted on plaster of Paris reconstructions of the decayed horns.

10 cm. This is large, as is the length of the horn (estimated from the 1939 excavation plans), and suggests that the horns came from a small post-glacial aurochs, an animal that Caesar describes the pre-Christian tribes as pursuing and trapping in almost ritual manner. Just as the Germani of the first century BC decorated their drinking horns with silver mounts so did their Anglian successors in the early seventh century AD.

The Sutton Hoo horns are mounted as a pair, with matching fittings of gilded silver foil. The lip of each horn is enclosed in a silver-gilt channelled rim band and immediately below the rim are four rectangular panels of silver, gilded so heavily that in places the gilding has separated from the silver as a distinct layer. The panels are impressed with a 51 complex design of six upright animals within bil-leted borders. The panels and the rim binding are held to the horn by silver-gilt clips in the form of double heads with moustachioed faces.

The body of the horns was left free of decorative fittings although they may have been painted or carved, but the solid ends carry a series of silver-gilt mounts and have bird-headed terminals with curv-ing predatory beaks, pointed chins and rectangular eye-surrounds enclosing beady eyes – details that are seen again on the birds of prey on the front of the shield, the purse-lid, the lyre and the great gold buckle.

The maplewood bottles are made as a set with 52 matching mounts of heavily gilded silver. The open mouth of each bottle is enclosed in a channelled binding held to the maplewood by three simple fluted strips that run the full depth of the upright neck and hold in place three rectangular panels of gilded silver foil that fill the neck. The panels are impressed with a bold design of two interlaced 51 horse-like animals with naturalistic heads with open jaws and pricked ears. Immediately below the neck panels, their top edge held beneath an ungilded and fluted silver band, lie nine triangular mounts or 'vandykes'. These have gilded fields within plain silver borders and are decorated with a pair of

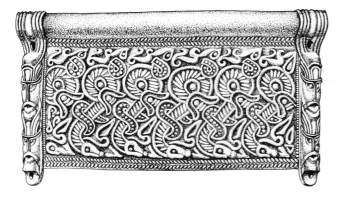

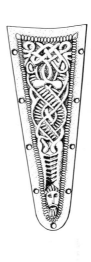

entwined ribbon animals whose front legs and jaws interlace at the top of the panel. The vandykes lie across the broad shoulder of the bottles and the more complete ones curve very slightly at the lower end reflecting the curve of the shoulder.

The horns show an astonishing range of decorative devices and techniques that are paralleled only by one other pair of horns, from the princely grave at Taplow in Buckinghamshire, which are mounted with a comparable series of decorative fittings. The maplewood bottles are also decorated with identical panels stamped with dies that were probably specially made and their closest parallels are also found in the Taplow burial. The similarities between the horns and bottles at Sutton Hoo and at Taplow

51 Reconstruction of the elegant animal ornament designs that decorated the mouth fittings of the drinking horns (left) and the maplewood bottles (right).

52 Replica of one of the bottles in maplewood with electrotype fittings.

strongly suggest that although the interlace decoration on the silver-gilt mounts of the Sutton Hoo horns and bottles has close links with Swedish animal ornament, the style of the horns and bottles must be Anglo-Saxon.

53 Group of walnut burwood cups mounted with neck fittings of silver and silver-gilt.

Eight burr-wood cups

Amongst the mass of small objects in the fluted silver bowl were four table knives with plain iron blades and bone handles, the little silver cup and a collection of eight small containers made from walnut burr-wood and decorated with silver and silver-gilt mounts. Two of these little cups have deep neck bands, each made up of three panels of gilded silver foil impressed with curious, closely

related designs of upright, but highly stylised animals with braceleted thighs and three-toed claw-like feet. The rims of the other cups are mounted with simpler fittings of silver and silver-gilt. The mounts are all held to the cups with tiny fluted clips in exactly the same way as the rim mounts of the maplewood bottles. It is not clear what these little cups were used for, although the use of walnut burr-wood together with simple, but costly, silver fittings suggests that they would have been highly prized. Their association in the fluted silver bowl with the silver cup and knives could suggest that they were used at table as small drinking vessels – perhaps not tot cups, as there is no evidence for the distillation of alcohol earlier than about 1100, but possibly for some special drink. Alternatively, the fact that the silver bowl also contained three combs could suggest that the cups were used for toilet purposes – perhaps as small storage jars for salves.

The gaming pieces

Amongst the rotting textiles in the Anastasius dish complex the excavators found a single gaming piece, placed separately it seems from its companions, as fragments of several others were found with the remains of the shield. The gaming piece, although badly decayed and impregnated with nodules of copper, still retained its shape. It was made of sperm whale ivory and was cylindrical with a slightly domed head. Its isolation from the other gaming pieces suggests that it had held some particular but undefinable importance for the dead man. The gaming pieces are a reminder that the Anglo-Saxons greatly enjoyed games involving counters or men and the remains of these are frequently found in Anglo-Saxon graves of all social levels; at Taplow, for example, a set of bone men with bronze rivets was laid at the dead man's feet. This pastime was no doubt inherited from the Germanic tribes who crossed over to Britain during and after the collapse of the Roman Empire and who were renowned for their passionate interest in gaming and gambling.

The musical instrument

The remains of the upper half of a round-headed lyre were found inside the bronze 'Coptic' bowl where they were protected from decay. From the fragments it has proved possible to reconstruct the upper half of the instrument. The wood used to build the lyre is maplewood – the same prized wood that was used for the bottles – and caught on many 54, 55 of the fragments were long shiny hairs which have been identified as beaver. These were found on fragments from both sides of the lyre and suggest that the instrument was buried, and perhaps kept, in a beaverskin bag.

The largest piece of the lyre to survive was the curved peg-arm. Although one end is badly shrunken and twisted, the other end is almost undistorted.

It held six pegs, five of willow and one of alder, around which gut or horsehair strings were wound. The ends of the peg-arm were shaped into flattened tenons that engage with mortices cut into the vertical arms of the sound-box. The joins were secured and disguised by gilt-bronze bird-headed escutcheons that were riveted through the wood and clenched over bronze washers on the back of the instrument. The construction of the sound-box is very simple: it is essentially a hollowed-out box with thin walls in the shape of the instrument, covered by a lid held to the box walls by tiny bronze pins. The pins, 9 mm long × 1 mm thick, are triangular and flat-sectioned and were cut from a narrow strip of bronze. The joints of the instrument may also have been glued but no evidence for this survives.

The escutcheons covering the joins between the peg-arm and the arms of the sound-box are made of heavily gilded bronze and consist of a square decorative panel with a bird-headed extension on the upper edge. The panel is filled with a circular band of cast zoomorphic interlace that encloses a centrally placed garnet setting. The corners of the plaques are filled with cloisonné settings containing three small, unevenly cut garnets. The escutcheons were slightly rebated into the wood and an impression on the undistorted end of the peg-arm shows that they were placed with the bird heads pointing upwards and inwards with their beaks following the curve of the peg-arm. The bird heads are of a type known as 'Germanic Style II', with pointed chins, curving beaks and an angular eye surround. The eye is formed from a raised bronze setting containing a flat garnet in an organic surround.

The lower part of the lyre is based entirely on the proportions and details of the very few surviving continental six-stringed instruments that are contemporary with the Sutton Hoo lyre, and on manuscript illustrations in the Vespasian Psalter and the Durham Cassiodorus which both show King David 56 playing a long straight-sided instrument with curving ends. Apart from the string pegs none of the fittings of the Sutton Hoo lyre survived inside the 'Coptic' bowl or immediately outside it and this suggests that although both bronze and amber bridges are known, the Sutton Hoo lyre bridge must have been made of bone, or perhaps ivory, which would have decayed in the acidic conditions of the burial chamber. The tail-piece for the strings and the button to which it was attached at the bottom of the

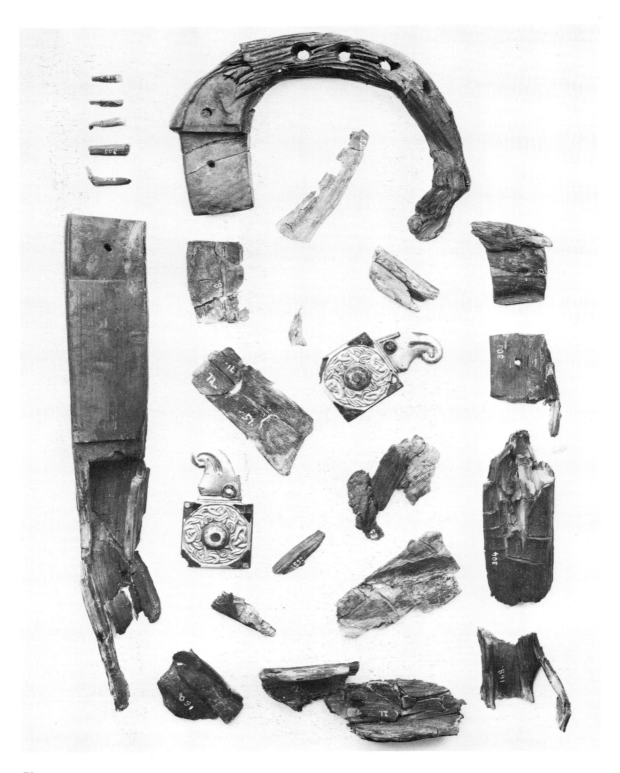

54 LEFT Fragments of maplewood, including the peg-arm, and the gilt-bronze bird-headed escutcheons from the lyre.

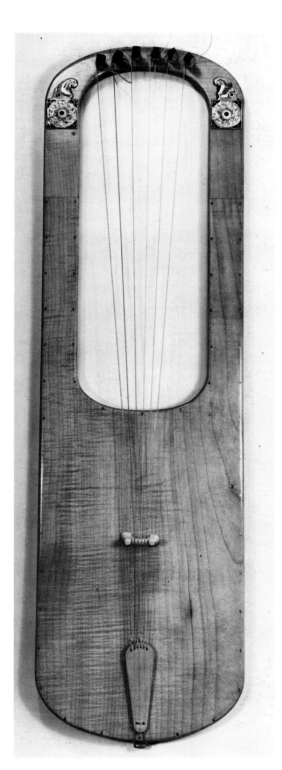
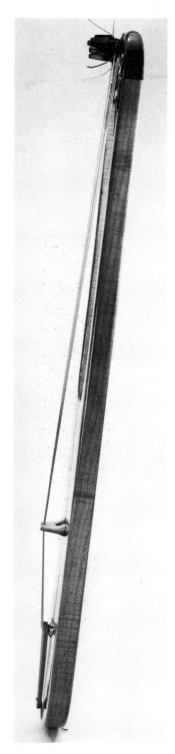

55 Reconstruction of the lyre, in maplewood with electrotype escutcheons. On the replica, the bridge is made of bone and the strings are gut. The side view shows the thickness of the instrument and the height of the bridge.

The hanging-bowls

Three bronze Celtic hanging-bowls with decorative escutcheons were placed in the grave in two groups like the silver. The largest, a magnificent bowl containing a fish raised on a bronze pedestal and decorated with superb enamelled escutcheons, was found inside the bronze 'Coptic' bowl at the west end of the chamber. An iron nail, rusted to one of its suspension rings, suggests that the bowl must have originally hung on the burial chamber wall immediately above the 'Coptic' bowl into which it fell either before or during the burial chamber collapse. The two small hanging-bowls were buried mouth down beneath a mass of textiles at the bottom of the Anastasius dish complex. Pl. II

The hanging-bowls are decorated in a tradition wholly different from the gold and garnet pieces in the Sutton Hoo burial. They belong to a family of bronze bowls that have their roots in the Celtic areas of the British Isles which are decorated with enamelled escutcheons filled with designs whose origins lie in the pre-Roman Iron Age and which survived largely untouched by the influence of Roman art. Hanging-bowls are mysterious in that their origins are not clear and their function is not fully understood, although they may perhaps have been used at table. They were highly prized and complete bowls or their decorative escutcheons are occasionally found in high-status graves in the Anglo-Saxon areas of England.

The large bowl (no. 1), perhaps the finest in the entire hanging-bowl series, is matched only by one other finely decorated bowl from Manton Common, Scunthorpe, which may have been made in the same workshop. The Sutton Hoo bowl is lightly made with a rim diameter of nearly 30 cm and a height of 13.5 cm. The thickness of the bronze is only 1 mm and it is not surprising that the bowl was repaired during its lifetime. The bowl has a flat out-turned rim with a thin bronze decorative strip soldered to it. Immediately below the cavetto are three hook escutcheons carrying bronze rings to which leather hanging straps were fitted. The hooks are in the form of stylised animal heads, perhaps seals, that peer over the rim into the depths of the bowl where an enamelled fish stands on a pedestal.

The escutcheons are decorated with Celtic scroll-work reserved in bronze against a pillar-box red champlevé field. Pieces of millefiori glass are also set in the red enamel. The escutcheons are surrounded by high frames made of a high-tin bronze

56 King David playing the lyre, from an eighth-century manuscript (Durham Cathedral Library).

instrument may have been made of either wood or bone.

Two reconstructions of the Sutton Hoo lyre have been made in the Dolmetsch workshops, in Haslemere, Surrey. Both are designed to play although one is kept purely for exhibition purposes. The second instrument is used by specialists in early music who have experimented both with the tuning intervals of the six strings and with different methods of playing it. The instrument is surprisingly resonant and would have provided excellent accompaniment both to songs and to the speaking of heroic poetry in the ambience of a king's hall.

57 The large hanging-bowl containing an
enamelled fish and repaired with silver
patches.

which gives them a slightly silvery appearance.
Below each hook escutcheon is a stylised Celtic
boar's head with deep eye sockets each filled with a
silver-gilt cell containing a flat garnet backed with
gold foil. This is an entirely non-Celtic technique
that must be the result of refurbishing in an English
workshop, the garnet eyes probably replacing pools
59 of enamel. Three square escutcheons are mounted
between and slightly below the hook escutcheons
on the maximum bulge of the bowl. They are also
enclosed by high-tin bronze frames and are decorated with scrolls and trisceles reserved in red
enamel and with millefiori glass.

The bowl has been repaired with three silver
patches. Two are small but the third is a large oval
patch decorated with an uncomfortable design of

two classic Style II bird heads, with curving beaks
and strong linear eye surrounds, joined by a
common box-like neck. Traces of gilding survive
and several random impressions of a triangular
waffle-patterned stamp lie near the bottom left-
hand edge of the patch. This patch is further
evidence that the bowl was extensively repaired in a
workshop which was producing Germanic style
objects.

A bronze fish rests on a slender pedestal inside 58
the bowl. It is badly damaged by corrosion but has
been identified as a member of the trout family. Its
body is decorated with inlaid spots of red enamel,
and fins, tail, gills and even incised scales survive.
Originally the upper half of the body was tinned so
that the fish would have had a silvery appearance.

73

58 The fish and pedestal mount from the large hanging-bowl. The pedestal rises from a flat, enamelled escutcheon and pierces the hollow body of the fish. The fish balances on the pedestal's broad shoulder and is free to spin at the touch of a finger.

59 One of the square escutcheons, decorated in Celtic style with a central field filled with pieces of millefiori glass. The four ovals of pale green enamel in the corners of the escutcheon contain slashes of red enamel.

60 Gilded silver patch with Style II birds' heads, with impressions of a small waffle stamp (bottom left), used to repair the large hanging-bowl.

61 The base of the medium hanging-bowl, mounted with an escutcheon decorated with a tinned swastika reserved in red enamel and enclosed by an applied bronze ring with foil-filled openings; enamelled hook escutcheon from the small hanging-bowl, containing a simple design of interlocking peltas reserved in a red enamel field.

Soldered to the outside of the bowl beneath the fish-escutcheon is a fifth and perfectly preserved circular escutcheon.

The small hanging-bowl (no. 3) belongs to the same decorative tradition as the first hanging-bowl but is insignificant in comparison. It is decorated with three boldly framed escutcheons with heavy and highly stylised animal-head hooks. The escutcheons are filled with red enamel containing a simple design of interlocking peltas. At the heart of the design is a single piece of millefiori glass.

The third hanging-bowl belongs to a different decorative tradition from the others. It has light escutcheons with stylised animal-head hooks. The escutcheons were not however enamelled but were decorated with bronze foil impressed with a balanced but obscure animal-based design. The bowl is mounted inside and out with a pair of basal escutcheons decorated with a four-headed swastika in tinned bronze reserved in red enamel. On the outside of the bowl is an openwork bronze ring that

originally contained five panels of bronze foil. A single openwork patch rises from the ring and this is also filled with foil.

Hanging-bowls were highly-prized objects and were carefully looked after and repaired. Their function is uncertain although it has been suggested that they may have held water for use at table.

Domestic containers

The Sutton Hoo ship-burial, like other rich graves, contained a wide range of objects to cover all aspects of the dead man's life in the afterworld, including a tub, three buckets and three cauldrons. Although essentially kitchen and storage equipment, the containers were all finished to a high standard and some perhaps came from the same workshop.

In many Anglo-Saxon graves offerings of food are placed in the containers but at Sutton Hoo no trace of fresh food such as fruit, nuts or grain survived, although there is highly complex evidence to suggest that a pile of burnt bones or a cooked joint may have been placed on the Anastasius dish (a royal

62 Reconstruction of the tub: the iron bands and decorative fittings are mounted on a fibreglass base. Flat silver escutcheons cover the rivet heads holding the handle-plates to the tub.

reflection perhaps of the find made in 1985 of a body accompanied by what appears to have been a very large joint of meat).

The burial party placed most of the containers along or on the east wall, well beyond the feet of the dead man. In the north-east corner lay the collapsed remains of a large yew-wood tub with the fragmentary iron bands of a straight-sided bucket inside. Next to the tub was an exceptionally large sheet-bronze cauldron (no. 1) which had been crushed during the collapse of the burial chamber. It lay partly over the tub close to a magnificent ornamental iron suspension chain. Mouth upwards on the chamber floor in the south-east corner were two smaller cauldrons with globular bodies that had been crushed flat, breaking into hundreds of tiny fragments that formed a halo of bronze around their iron mouth fittings.

Not all the containers were laid out along the east wall: one yew-wood bucket (no. 3) was centrally placed at the west end of the chamber among objects that have a quite different connotation from the finds at the opposite end. The third bucket (no. 2), probably also of yew, was placed in isolation on the southern edge of the chamber floor where it had collapsed across strakes 5 and 6 because of the slight list of the ship. At the eastern end of the central deposit were two other small domestic objects. One, an iron lamp, had been filled with beeswax and could have provided a rather feeble light inside the chamber. The other was a narrow-necked pottery bottle, which can only have been valued for its contents, of which no trace survived.

The tubs and buckets

The tub and three buckets are all built like a modern barrel with wooden staves held together by a series of iron bands. The tub is massively built with splaying sides and a rim diameter of 51 cm. Its original height is uncertain but it has been reconstructed with the rim 52 cm above floor level. It is raised off the ground on three small iron feet. The buckets are straight-sided with approximate diameters of 22 cm, 25 cm and 33 cm. They are too fragmentary for any accurate assessment of their height to be made, but a reasonably proportioned reconstruction of bucket 3 has been made with a height of 33 cm.

The mouth of each vessel is mounted with a broad iron band that is clamped to the staves by a channelled iron strip. The strip fully encloses the tops of the staves and is itself held securely in position by a series of iron clips that hook over the rim and are riveted through the mouth band and the staves. On the tub they are hidden by large flat silver escutcheons, while on the buckets small bronze escutcheons are used instead. The rim clips on the tub and buckets 1 and 3 develop branching finials that curve into simplified but elegant bird-headed terminals, with the birds' eyes defined by the dome-headed rivets that hold the terminals to the staves. In contrast, the clips on bucket 2 extend as simple twisted rods.

Different methods were used to carry the tub and the three buckets. The tub, probably because of its size and weight when full, was fitted with two heavy iron ring handles and was carried slung from

63 Reconstruction of bucket 3 which lay at the west end of the chamber.

a pole by two or more people. With a capacity of about 100 litres it would have been exceptionally heavy and awkward to manage when full and it may well have been used largely as a storage vessel from which smaller containers like the buckets were filled. The buckets, in contrast, had bailed handles exactly like their modern counterparts.

Although the method of carrying the tub is different from that of the three buckets, the system used to attach the handles and carrying rings to the vessels is the same: opposing pairs of iron handle plates with decorative finials were riveted onto the containers at rim level. All the rivet heads were disguised by decorative escutcheons.

The cauldrons

When the excavators uncovered the objects at the east end of the burial chamber, they found large

64 The east end of the burial chamber: to the left are the remains of the bronze cauldrons, the iron-bound tub and the chainwork. The Anastasius dish, lying partially over the fluted silver bowl, is above the metre scale.

fragments of bronze partially overlying the collapsed tub. This bronze was the remains of a remarkably large cauldron with iron fittings that had apparently been hung up by one of its large drop handles so that its mouth lay against the burial chamber wall. Although crushed flat in the collapse of the chamber, much of the bronze survived in large sheets so that its original dimensions can be established. It has a diameter of 70 cm, an overall height of 34 cm and a capacity of just under 100 litres. It hung from two large iron rings which would have engaged the pot-hooks of a suspension chain. The rim is mounted at equal intervals with four scroll-ended iron strips riveted through holes

crudely punched in the rim to an iron supporting strip below. The strips are placed opposite the handles and at the point of maximum strain between them so that when the cauldron was lifted or hung from a chain they would prevent the rim from buckling.

Technically the cauldron is a remarkable example of the metalworker's skill as it is raised from a single sheet of bronze. Its walls are on average only 1.2 mm thick and the surface still shows impressions of the planishing hammer rising in a carefully controlled spiral from the centre of the curved base where there is a hole with a diameter of 11 mm. This could perhaps be a drainage hole although no trace of a bung survived.

The only parallel to this large bronze cauldron was found in the Taplow grave (BM, MLA 83,12-14,9). The cauldrons are so similar in design and execution that it is possible that they may have been made in the same workshop although their dates of burial are two or three decades apart. Their origins lie in the composite cauldrons of the Roman period, where sheets of bronze were riveted together to form the vessel in a tradition that had remained unchanged since the first composite cauldrons of the late Bronze Age.

Two smaller cauldrons lay immediately south of the large cauldron but only their necks and rims survived in reasonably large fragments. Cauldron 2 has a mouth diameter of approximately 40 cm and cauldron 3 is slightly smaller; their capacities are impossible to estimate. Both were equipped with bailed iron handles that hook onto upright triangular lugs that develop from the flat, outturned rim. The cauldrons belong to a distinctive family of round-bellied and carinated bronze vessels that are widely distributed across northern Europe and Scandinavia.

65 The much-damaged remains of the large bronze cauldron with heavily corroded iron ring handles. The walls fall straight to the carination, which forms a distinct ledge, suggesting that the cauldron may have rested in an iron frame when not supported over a fire.

The chainwork

Associated with cauldron 1, but not attached to it, was a magnificent iron suspension chain. It had been placed between the cauldron and the eastern end of the central deposit and survived as an untidy coil of corroded links with its large suspension ring at a lower level than the two pot-hooks. Traces of three different textiles show that the ring was in contact with the textiles while it was corroding and that it did not hang from the timber frame of the burial chamber.

Despite corrosion the designs of the individual elements survive and have been recovered by radiography. Reconstruction drawings based on the radiographs show some of the design skills of the smiths who created the chain, and the making of a modern version in the early 1970s by a master blacksmith, H.C. Landon, and his brother stretched their smithing abilities to the utmost.

The chain is 3.45 m long and would have hung from a cross-beam in the roof of a substantial timber-hall – with a cauldron attached to it as large as cauldron 1 it would have needed a beam height

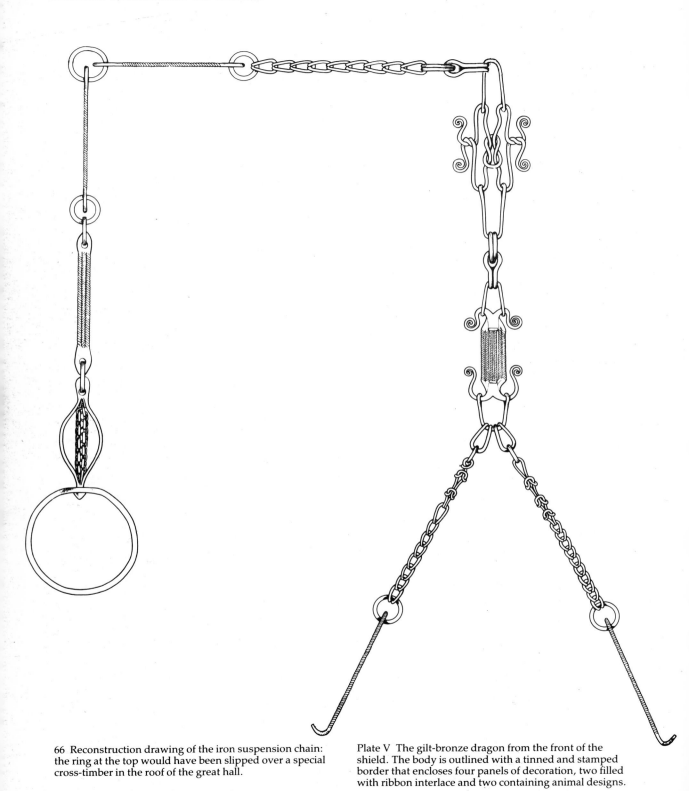

66 Reconstruction drawing of the iron suspension chain: the ring at the top would have been slipped over a special cross-timber in the roof of the great hall.

Plate V The gilt-bronze dragon from the front of the shield. The body is outlined with a tinned and stamped border that encloses four panels of decoration, two filled with ribbon interlace and two containing animal designs.

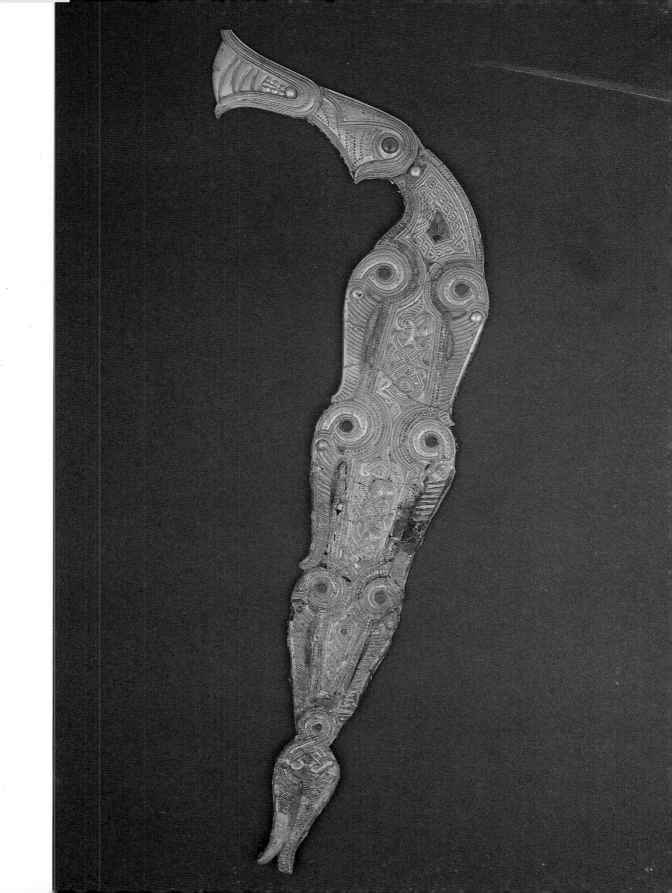

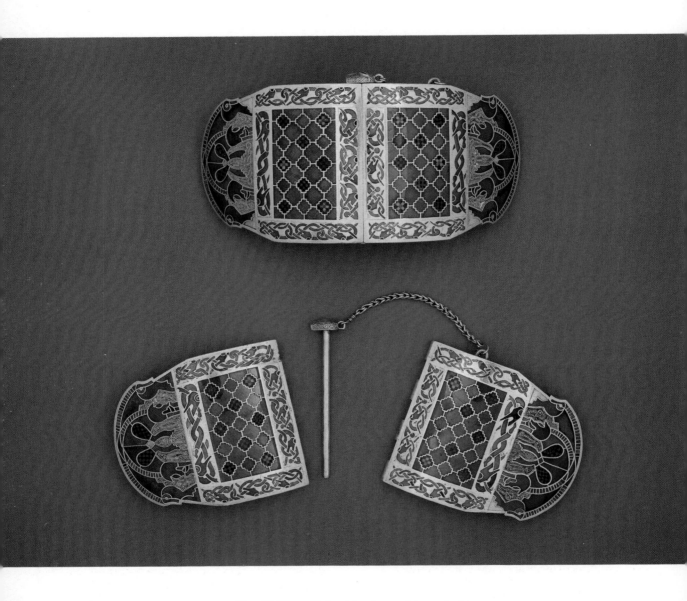

Plate VI The gold shoulder-clasps, decorated with
cloisonné garnets and millefiori glass. The curved ends
contain a complex design of two interlacing boars.

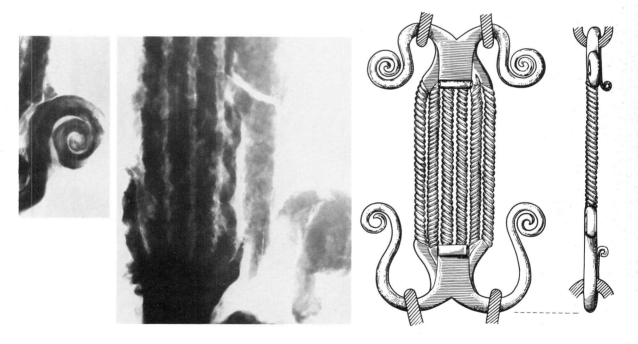

67 TOP Modern re-creation of the Sutton Hoo chain showing the complexity of the elements. The end of the top element runs through a specially expanded area in the iron ring and is burred over to form a conical stop so that the chain is free to turn.

68 An element of the chain, made up of six parallel cables, each containing four wires twisted together in opposite directions to form a complex herringbone pattern. The cable-ends are hammered into plates with curlicued terminals. The radiographs show how the details of the design are hidden in the iron corrosion.

of at least 5 m. The chain fell from a massive ring to which it was attached by a swivel so that the cauldron could rotate slowly without the chain twisting. Its main length is formed of seven complex elements joined by simple rings or U-shaped links. At the lower end it divides into two chain-link arms each with a hefty pot-hook which would engage the drop-ring handles of a large cauldron. Because of the murky smoke-laden atmosphere in any building at this time, the smith who made the chain placed the most decorative elements towards the lower end where they could be seen.

The iron lamp and pottery bottle

A little way from the material along the east wall were two small and rather homely objects – a lamp and a small bottle. The lamp consists of a cup-shaped iron bowl supported in a cage of three iron straps clamped beneath the bowl by an iron neckband. Below this the straps emerge as widely splaying legs with spatulate feet that provide a stable base. When excavated the lamp still contained a lump of beeswax but no trace of a wick remained. Undistinguished in appearance, the lamp is extremely unusual and has only one surviving parallel in Anglo-Saxon archaeology, in a high-status grave at Broomfield in Essex (BM, MLA 94, 12–16, 15). No other all-iron lamps are known, but the find of a tripod stand, which may perhaps have held a wooden bowl that could have been filled with beeswax and used as a lamp, may explain why so few lamps have survived from the Anglo-Saxon period.

Lying on its side close to the lamp was a small bottle made of a buff-coloured clay. The bottle stands just over 15 cm high with a maximum girth of 8 cm. It has a flat base and a conical body, decorated with three shallow grooves, which narrows into a long neck with an everted rim. Inside is an oblique stain, presumably made by its slowly evaporating contents after it had toppled over onto its side. As the bottle is unglazed it would have been suitable only for viscous liquids, unless it had been lined with a substance like resin to reduce its porosity. Its presence in the burial is something of a mystery as the dead man was provided with a sumptuous range of containers and drinking vessels, but as it lay on the edge of the Anastasius dish complex where small personal objects were placed it may have held a personal significance for him.

69 The iron lamp, which still contains its fuel in the form of solidified beeswax.

70 The pottery bottle, which would only have been suitable for holding contents like thin honey unless it had been lined with resin. Alternatively, it may have held something originally in powder or granule form that combined with the dampness in the burial chamber to stain the inside of the bottle.

9 Symbols of power

The 'sceptre'

Apart from the royal regalia discussed later in this chapter, the symbols of power in the Sutton Hoo ship-burial are thought to be contained within two enigmatic objects, a 'sceptre' and a stand, whose function is still not fully understood and may never be. In the Classical world the sceptre is a readily identifiable object usually in the form of a rod with a decorative terminal but at Sutton Hoo the power of the dead king seems to have been vested in a wholly barbaric object that perhaps contains a totemic significance.

The Sutton Hoo 'sceptre' was found lying parallel to the west wall of the burial chamber, a little way in from it and close to the stand. It is made of two distinct elements – a massive whetstone and a delicately modelled bronze stag.

Pl. I

The sharpening planes of the four-sided whetstone show no sign of use and it was presumably a symbolic device representing the power of the sword sharpener. The fine-grained stone is delicately carved at either end with a series of sombre faces, some with beards, others clean-shaven, in pear-shaped borders that develop at the bottom into a small flat disc. At each end above the faces the stone constricts sharply and then expands into a red-painted knop enclosed in a bronze cage. The proportions of the knops are slightly different: the upper is rather squat and the lower is more elongated, presumably to balance differently designed fittings.

When the whetstone was excavated the fitting from its upper end was missing. Nothing was found during the 1939 excavations or during the re-excavations of 1965–70 that could be associated with a small bronze fitting similar to the cup-like rest at its lower end and it is thought that the missing terminal is the small bronze stag that lay close to the whetstone alongside the cage of the iron stand. The stag is cast in bronze and is beautifully modelled, combining a realistic head with a stylised body and legs. Identified as a red deer, it is crowned with a full set of antlers that surprisingly survived almost intact. The stag is mounted on a ring made of twisted iron wires that fits into a collared bronze T-shaped element. This in turn fits into a bronze

71 The stone 'sceptre'.

72 Detail of the lower end of the whetstone, showing one of the finely modelled bearded faces and the bronze cage-like fitting that may have acted as a rest for the 'sceptre'.

73 The bronze stag and iron-wire ring from the top of the whetstone. Radiography suggests that the collared T-shaped bronze element holding the ends of the ring simply rested in the pedestal, so that the stag and ring could be rotated – and perhaps even removed from the whetstone.

pedestal-base so that the stag and ring are free to turn in much the same way as the fish in the large hanging-bowl. Sculpture in the round is extremely rare in early Anglo-Saxon England: apart from the stylised boar figures from Guilden Morden in Cambridgeshire and from a helmet found at Benty Grange, Staffordshire, and the seated man from the lid of a cremation urn excavated at Spong Hill,

Norfolk, the only other examples, both in bronze, are the stag and fish from Sutton Hoo.

The 'sceptre' is an object that has no parallel in European or Scandinavian archaeology. Its two incompatible elements make up a formidably impressive object that is essentially barbaric in conception, owing nothing to classical counterparts portrayed in ivories, manuscripts or mosaics. It may be possible that the eight delicately carved faces, each with a decided individuality, are ancestral portraits perhaps of the Wuffinga tribe to which the ruling caste of the East Anglian kingdom belonged. If so, the whetstone may have been vested with a totemic significance that cannot easily be translated into modern concepts. Whetstones with carved terminals are known from occasional finds in Ireland, Wales, Scotland and northern England, where they are almost always decorated with a single head. None, however, displays the sculptural virtuosity of the Sutton Hoo stone or the barbaric grandeur of its red-painted knops.

The stand

A second object in the Sutton Hoo ship-burial perhaps associated with the temporal power of the 74 dead man is the iron stand. Like the sceptre it is an object with no parallels whose significance and function can never be fully understood. It was found lying along the west wall of the burial chamber close to the whetstone and stag.

The design of the stand is extraordinary and is composed of a square-sectioned iron rod, 172 cm tall, to which is forged a cage. This is made of four twisted iron rods that fall from the corners of a grille placed towards the top of the central shaft. The grille, made of iron strips, closely resembles the cooking grids that are occasionally found in continental and Scandinavian contexts. At each corner the strips are fashioned into a stylised animal head with long curving horns. The lower end of the shaft is forged into a foot by splitting iron away from the sides of the shaft and curling it over to form volutes. The foot, although short, may have been designed to be stamped into the ground to support the stand upright. It may also be a decorative device to complete the lower end of the shaft, balancing the otherwise top-heavy cage.

When the stand was first excavated various suggestions were put forward for its use – it was thought that it might have been a flambeau, and that pieces of oil-soaked cloth might have been wrapped around the grille and then set alight. Another suggestion was that the grille might have been filled with feathers or streamers of brightly coloured cloth. A third suggestion identifies it as a ship's weather vane. The general consensus however is that as it was buried in a royal grave in close association with the stag and whetstone, it must in some way be connected with the symbols of power

that are common to all rulers. Bede, writing of Edwin, king of Northumbria, describes how banners were carried before him in battle and in times of peace, and how his standard-bearer preceded him when he moved around his kingdom. Bede also makes a direct reference to a specific type of banner or standard, the tufa (*tuuf*), and it is clear that in Northumbria at least the bearing of standards before the king was well established. But does the Sutton Hoo stand belong in this category, or is it part of the royal regalia of East Anglia? The stand is top-heavy and difficult to hold and it may perhaps have been carried with its foot in a leather frog, in much the same way as modern regimental colours. It could equally well have been driven into the ground or wedged upright in a large block of wood and seen together with the sceptre on ceremonial occasions as a symbol of authority and power. With no direct documentary evidence, and no parallels, the interpretation of the stand can never be more than theoretical and it will perhaps always remain an enigma.

The regalia

When the Sutton Hoo ship burial was excavated it was immediately identified as a royal grave because of the astonishing quality and quantity of gold and garnet jewellery that had been placed in it. The jewellery, perhaps the work of master craftsmen commissioned by a royal patron, falls into two groups, one of fittings belonging to the sword and sword belt, the other a group consisting of four major works of art that can be loosely termed as regalia. This group, although constantly referred to as jewellery and highly decorative, is strictly functional. It is made up of a pair of hinged shoulder-clasps, the lid of a decayed leather purse that contained a collection of small gold coins from Merovingian Gaul and a massive gold belt buckle.

Although no trace of a body was found in the burial chamber the placing of the gold and garnet 75 pieces has an overall logic which suggests that they were worn in the grave. It is possible to imagine the dead man laid out in the burial chamber, perhaps slightly raised above the floor on a low platform, wearing a leather cuirass fastened at shoulder-level by magnificent gold and garnet clasps and around his waist a broad belt held by a large gold buckle. From this a leather purse with a jewelled lid hung from three small straps. The regalia is

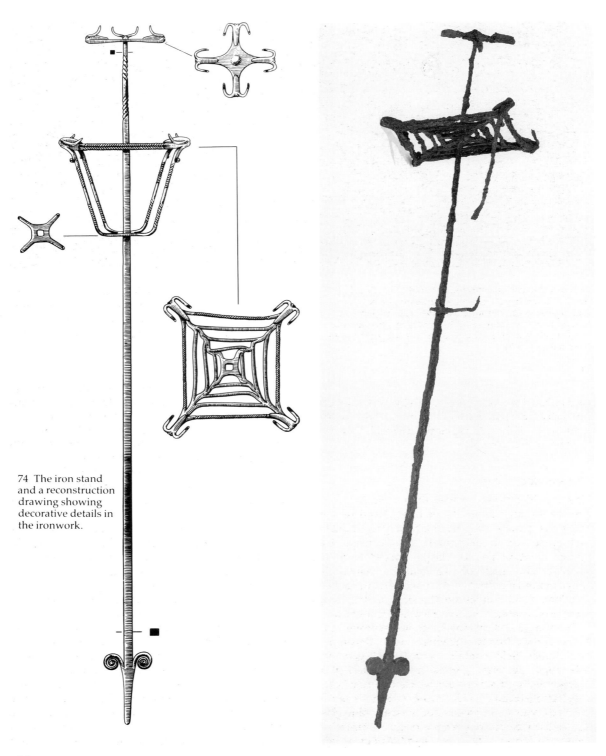

74 The iron stand
and a reconstruction
drawing showing
decorative details in
the ironwork.

75 The principal concentration of gold finds, 22 July 1939: (from left to right) the scabbard slider and three rectangular mounts from the sword belt; the purse-lid, face down in the sand, with the gold coins, blanks and billets spilling over the frame; the great gold buckle and the small gold slider.

unparalleled in its richness, mechanical ingenuity and artistic design, although the purse-lid and great gold buckle belong to types that are well-known in Europe at this time.

The shoulder-clasps

76, Pl. VI The shoulder-clasps, whose origins lie in Roman prototypes, are unique. Made of gold and set with cloisonné garnets, they are completely functional as well as supremely decorative. They consist of an almost identical pair of clasps, curved to fit the shoulder and made of two matching halves that hinge around a central gold pin with an animal head terminal. Gold staples on the back of the clasps were used to attach them to a leather over-garment.

The shoulder-clasps share a common design: each half is divided into two distinct zones of decoration. Each inner field contains a balanced geometric scheme in cloisonné garnets and millefiori glass, surrounded by four narrow panels of animal orna- ment also executed in cloisonné garnets except for the eyes, which are picked out in bright blue glass. The ends of the clasps are curved and contain a bold cloisonné design of two entwined boars using large

garnets and slabs of millefiori glass. Small garnets are used to pick out details of the spine, the curled tail, the jaws and the tusks and gold filigree is used to fill the gaps between the boars' heads and legs.

The purse-lid

The purse-lid combines similar artistic display and Pl. VIII mechanical ingenuity and also shares stylistic links and workshop techniques with the shoulder-clasps. It consists of a kidney-shaped base of bone or ivory that is enclosed by a two-piece gold frame set with garnets and millefiori glass. At the top is a straight bar to which three hinges are soldered. These act as suspension points for thin straps that attach the purse to the waist belt and as hinges on which the purse opens.

The lower part of the frame is curved and in the middle is soldered the tongue of a catch to lock the purse. This engages a gold fitting that works on a sliding principle: the tongue is pushed into the catch which is then moved sideways so that when it is centred on the purse frame the tongue cannot be disengaged and the purse is locked.

Within the frame, set proud of the lid, are seven decorative plaques. Two of these are hexagonal and filled with a complex small-scale design in cloisonné garnets. Between them is an irregularly shaped plaque containing a complex design of four inter- laced animals with spines and hips picked out in small square garnets – the same technique used on the shoulder-clasps to emphasise the details of the entwined boars. The lower half of the purse-lid is

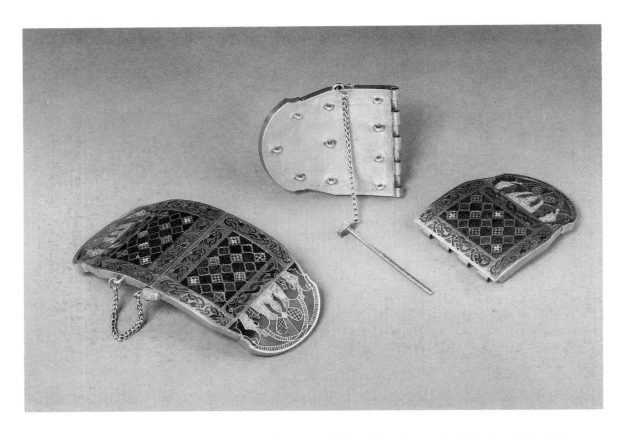

set with four figural plaques, two containing identical designs of a man standing between two wolf-like animals and two mirror image designs of a bird with a cruelly curved beak stooping on its prey. Like the boar designs on the shoulder-clasps these plaques use large areas of cloisonné garnets and chequerboard millefiori glass to contrast with the small square-cut garnets used for the feathers of the birds' wings and tails and the eye surround of the hunting birds. On the purse-lid undecorated areas of gold are also used to emphasise the design so that the overall impact is not lost by using only inlays of garnet and glass. The gold is not however solid but made up of carefully shaped cells lidded with thin gold sheet.

The coins

Inside the leather purse was a collection of 37 tiny gold coins, three unstruck gold blanks and two small gold billets. The coins (all tremisses from Merovingian Gaul) had been minted between 575

76 The gold and garnet shoulder-clasps. The tightly-fitting hinges are recessed so that they do not interrupt the overall decorative scheme when the clasps are fastened. The pin heads are in the form of animal heads with lentoid eyes and are decorated with filigree rings.

and 625 and had clearly been carefully selected to form a collection as each one had been made at a different mint. They are of great importance to the archaeologist as the date of the latest coins, or a little after to allow for their collection, must suggest the earliest possible date that the burial could have taken place. In the early seventh century, East Anglia did not have a coin-based economy and this suggests that the coins were placed in the grave for some specific purpose. In the context of a royal burial they do not represent a great deal of wealth and as they are quite clearly a deliberately selected group and not a random handful from a royal treasury it may be that they were placed in the grave to symbolise the conviction of the living that the dead must pay for their crossing to the after life. This belief can occasionally be seen in high-status

77 Obverse of one of the Merovingian tremisses (no. 26) from the purse, with a diademed and draped bust. The coin was minted at Valence (Drôme) between 595 and 605.

78 The reverse of coin 9, showing a Latin cross flanked by two smaller equal-armed crosses. The mint is uncertain but it may have been in the Limoges area. The coin was minted between 605 and 615.

Anglo-Saxon inhumations where small gold coins are found in the mouths of the dead. This practice is interpreted as a barbarian adoption of the obol that was paid to Charon to ferry the dead across the river Styx to the underworld – a belief that is part of classical mythology. None the less a similar super-stition seems to have been an accepted part of Anglo-Saxon ritual. Such payment in gold may perhaps be relevant to the placing of the coins in the ship-burial and it has been suggested that their strangely specific number – 37 coins and 3 coin-sized blanks – could perhaps be payment for the 40 oarsmen who would have carried the dead king to his next life and that the two gold billets would then be a suitable fee for the steersman upon whose guidance the ship depended for a successful land-fall. It is of course impossible for archaeologists to verify this and it may equally well be true that the number of coins does not have an especial signi-ficance and that their presence in the grave repre-sents nothing more than purchasing power: a symbol of the king's wealth and as such a guarantee

of high status in much the same way as the helmet and shield are symbols of his warrior status, or the sceptre is a symbol of his temporal power.

The great gold buckle

Lying close to the purse-lid, face up in the ground was a magnificent gold buckle – the buckle that held Pl. VII the broad belt from which the purse hung. This buckle is another piece of metalwork that is artisti-cally unparalleled despite its purely functional nature. It is very large and weighs 412.7 g. Unlike the other belt fittings in the burial (which are constructed of a substantial front plate and a thin back plate) it is made of two box-like elements. The buckle opens on a concealed hinge above the shoulders and is locked by an intricate system that shows the ingenuity of the master craftsman who created it: the back of the buckle is pierced by three 79 narrow rectangular slots that house short necks which connect thick flat sliders on the outside of the back plate to small oval plates, each with a project-

79 The back of the gold buckle,
showing the three sliders that are part
of the locking mechanism; and side
view of the opened buckle: the tips of
the shanks that engage the locking pins
can just be seen.

ing pin, inside the buckle. When the buckle is closed, the sliders can be moved towards each other so that the tips of the pins run through holes cut in the long shanks of the three bosses that dominate the display surface of the buckle and lock it. The end of the belt would have been fed into the open buckle and slots cut into it would enable the rods of the locking mechanism to engage so that when the buckle was closed the walls would hold the leather firm. The other end of the belt, cut down to form a tongue, would have been threaded through the buckle loop and held by the moulded tongue.

Although the buckle is essentially functional it is also one of the most superbly decorated objects in the burial. The display surfaces are decorated all over with a combination of different animal- and bird-based designs that are an exquisitely controlled display of one of the most ingenious art styles flourishing in the late sixth and early seventh centuries – Germanic Style II.

The ornament was cast and then worked up and finished with a variety of punched decoration whose recessed fields are filled with niello so that the designs stand out against the bland surface of the gold. Different punches are used to emphasise

different areas of the surface and details are also textured by pecking the smooth surface of the gold with a sharp point. In contrast to this surface detail, areas are left unstamped – the birds' beaks, the paws of the interlaced animals, the three large bosses and the little crouching beast at the foot of the buckle – in a way that emphasises the control that the goldsmith had over the totality of the design.

The great gold buckle belongs to a well-defined family of large buckles of gold, bronze and iron, often inlaid with silver interlace in geometric patterns imitating cloisonné cell-work. The Sutton Hoo buckle however is the grandest of the type, whose distribution extends from eastern England to the Rhine. It is yet another example of the transformation of contemporary mainstream types into something extraordinary in the hands of a master craftsman working to a royal commission.

Six strap-mounts

Lying amongst the fittings from the sword and purse belts were a group of gold and cloisonné garnet strap fittings. Five of these may have been

80 Gold and garnet fittings from subsidiary belts and straps (from left to right): triangular mount or strap-distributor; matching buckle- and strap-mounts with curved ends decorated with large garnets in simple cell shapes; small gold slider and strap-end.

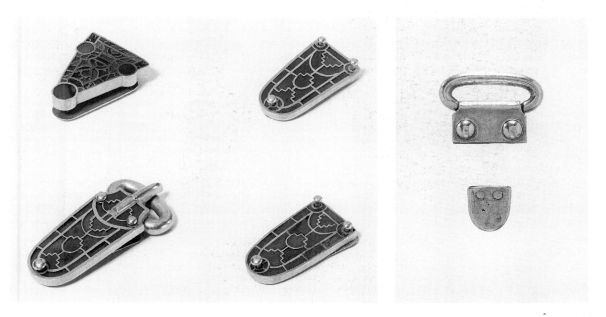

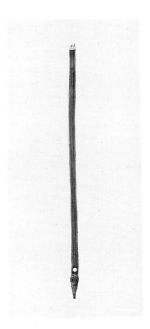

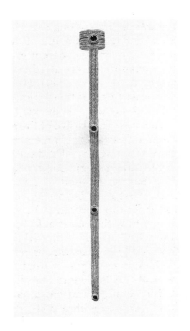

81 Five gold fittings that may have been mounted on a
bone or ivory wand: sheet-gold wolf (left, above), curved
for attachment to the wand; (below) triangular mount
lightly engraved with a pair of animals; fluted strip with
an animal-head terminal and ring-headed filigree strip set
with cabochon garnets in raised collared settings.

attached to a strap that ran across the body and over
the shoulder to support the purse-belt. Three form a
set of a small buckle and two strap-mounts and are
decorated with simple cell-shapes. They are held to
their strap by three dome-headed gold rivets
clenched over a thin backplate of gold sheet. Although the garnets used in the buckle and strap-
mounts are considerably larger than those used in
the sword-belt mounts (compare figs 26 and 80) the
standard of workmanship is still exceptionally high
and the simplicity of design makes them stand out
in contrast to the small-scale design of the sword-
belt mounts.

Lying close to the great gold buckle and probably
also associated with the support strap for the purse-
belt was a small, undecorated gold slider and a plain
gold fitting for the tongue of a strap.

A fourth gold and cloisonné garnet mount that
matches none of the other belt fittings was also
found close to the nucleus of the sword-belt fittings.
The mount is triangular and its function is uncertain
– it could be a decorative mount from a thick strap
or a distributor lying at the junction of two average

or three thin straps. It is sturdily made and decorated with a fussy design in very poorly executed
cloisonné garnet work. The poor workmanship of
this mount sets it aside from all the other cloisonné
pieces in the Sutton Hoo burial and it has been
suggested that it is a piece made by an apprentice to
the Sutton Hoo master, but it could equally well be a
piece from a less competent workshop.

The wand

Although the Sutton Hoo ship-burial is principally
known for its magnificent gold and garnet jewellery, there are several smaller pieces from the
metalsmith's workshop which are often overlooked.
The most interesting of these is a group of five
delicate gold fittings made up of two strips, two
zoomorphic mounts and a single cabochon garnet
setting.

The fittings were all found in the same small area
as the sword-belt mounts, with the exception of the
major piece, a filigree strip set with cabochon
garnets which was found lying across the sword

blade, and a matching cabochon setting which lay immediately to the south of the sword. The five do not form a single coherent group and it is still not clear what they were attached to, or even if they all belong to the same object. However it does seem as if at least three of them were attached to a pencil-thin rod – perhaps some kind of wand.

The most impressive of the five objects is a finely-made ring-headed filigree strip set with cabochon garnets in filigree collared settings which match the single setting found south of the sword blade. The strip has no method of attachment and the ring head must have been slipped over the end of the rod it was to decorate. The rod was also possibly mounted with a sheet gold fitting in the shape of a tiny wolf that was wrapped around the wand and fastened to it by gold nails that pierce its paws.

The two other pieces from the group belong less certainly to the same object. The second strip is delicately made and has a narrow stylised animal-head terminal with a pointed snout and tiny eyes that are pricked in the smooth surface of the gold. Immediately behind the head is a single hole for nailing the strip to whatever it originally decorated. The fifth piece is a tiny triangular mount of sheet gold incised with a pair of animals. The mount was originally curved but it is too battered for the degree of curve to be estimated. It was held by two nails to the object on which it was mounted.

The mounts pose two major questions: were they all mounted on the same object and what was this made of? It was clearly solid as it was capable of being pierced by nails and must have been organic in origin as no trace of it survived. One clue may be given by the survival of a patch of sand with a remarkably high phosphate content inside the ring-head of the filigree strip, which would suggest that the rod was made of bone or ivory rather than wood. But if the mounts do represent the fittings of a delicate bone or ivory wand, how should this be interpreted? Can so fine a rod be a symbol of office of some kind, similar to the more substantial examples seen on some of the ivories of the early Christian period, or did the wand have some other significance that is now lost? It has no convincing parallels and remains an enigma.

3 Modern Times

10 Treasure trove?

The fate of the Sutton Hoo treasure was debated at the coroner's court held in the village hall at Sutton on 14 August 1939. Fourteen jurors found that the gold and silver in the ship-burial was not treasure trove but the property of the landowner, Mrs Edith Pretty. In English law when gold, silver-plate or bullion is found hidden in the ground (buried with the intent to recover it) and the owner is unknown, it is declared treasure trove and belongs to the Crown. If for example a hoard of silver is buried by its owner with the intention of recovering it, and if the owner is subsequently prevented from digging it up again so that the silver is abandoned and becomes ownerless, it can be claimed as treasure trove. Sutton Hoo was an unusual case as the treasure was placed publicly in a grave accompanying a human burial and with no intention of recovery. Under such circumstances gold or silver may not be treasure trove and so can become the property of the landowner.

The award of the gold and silver in the ship-burial to Mrs Pretty was a controversial decision and there were moves to challenge it by the Crown, but these were allayed when Mrs Pretty gave the contents of the ship-burial to the nation. The Crown's challenge would presumably have been based on the fact that since the thirteenth century, treasure, especially from barrows, had been the property of the King and licences to dig for treasure were frequently granted – for example Dr Dee was licensed by Elizabeth I to dig for treasure in Suffolk. However, the decision to award the Sutton Hoo treasure to Mrs Pretty was not challenged and has been followed subsequently (Winchester 1971), but this kind of decision over treasure as part of a human burial is rare and stands outside the usual treasure trove procedures. Any future case involving a treasure buried in a similar fashion could perhaps challenge the Sutton Hoo ruling.

The ownership of the mounds and their finds remained with Mrs Pretty until her death in 1942 when by the terms of her will the rights to excavate were handed to her son, as was the right to retain any finds made in subsequent excavations.

When the war ended the British Museum embarked on a programme of research and restoration under the direction of Dr Rupert Bruce-Mitford who published the Museum's first guide to the ship burial in 1947. The quality and complexity of the finds demanded the resources of a specialist team of archaeologists, historians and conservators who worked for twenty years on a comprehensive catalogue published in three volumes in 1975, 1978 and 1983. The results of their research and interpretation, and the new questions which it raised, are discussed in the following chapters.

Plate VII The great gold buckle, decorated with interlacing animal ornament.
83 The scene at the treasure trove inquest in the village hall at Sutton in August 1939.

11 Restoration work

When the finds were brought back to the Museum after the war, the slow process of unpacking began, together with restoration of the major objects in preparation for the first public display of the treasure. The Anastasius dish which had been crushed down onto its deep foot-ring was straightened out by a combination of heating with a blow torch and judicious hammering, while the larger fragments of the helmet were assembled onto a sculptured plaster head; the fragile silver-gilt neck mounts and 'vandykes' from the drinking-horn complex were glued onto silk netting and the most complete were assembled onto one gigantic drinking horn and two smaller ones. At the same time the shield was restored with the bird and dragon above and below the central boss and the lyre was reconstructed as a small square harp.

These restorations, completed by 1948, survived for over twenty years but during that time research on the grave and its parallels had begun to throw doubt on their accuracy: the size of the great horn, for example, was found to be based on an animal that had been extinct in Europe since the end of the Ice Age! When eventually a combined research and conservation team was established to work on Sutton Hoo finds it was decided to dismantle the suspect restorations and to begin work again on the fragments and their residues that had been lifted with them in 1939 and still remained labelled in their original boxes. It had also become possible to recapture something of the original appearance of some of the more complicated objects from blown-up excavation photographs and these provided vital clues especially for the reconstruction of the shield and for the objects in the drinking-horn complex – one of the most complicated groups in the burial.

The drinking-horn complex

The silver-gilt mounts in the drinking-horn complex had been assembled into one large and two small drinking horns, but the validity of the large horn had been disproved and the excavation plans and photographs showed that two horn terminals had been found. The three horns were dismantled and the rim panels and 'vandykes' from the giant horn were reassembled onto models of a horn belonging

to a smaller aurochs that was alive in Europe until the seventeenth century. A problem was then posed by the smaller set of silver-gilt foil fittings. If the mounts from the large horn came from two smaller ones what did the panels and 'vandykes' on the original small horns belong to? Fragments of foil in the reserve collections suggested that there were enough panels and 'vandykes' to furnish several objects – could these be even smaller horns or did the mounts belong to some other so far unidentified object?

Excavation photographs provided the first clue. They showed quite clearly that the 'vandykes' lay spread out like the arms of a starfish and this suggested that they must originally have been

84 The crushed remains of the maplewood bottles: the triangular shapes of silver-gilt 'vandykes' can be seen surrounding the circular gilt-bronze rim-fitting. The complex was lifted in sections and not investigated in the field.

Plate VIII The purse-lid: the gold frame is set with cloisonné garnets and millefiori glass and encloses a modern lid containing the gold, garnet and millefiori plaques.

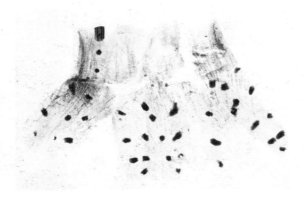

85 Fragments of maplewood impressed with the designs of the animal ornament from the silver-gilt fittings, and a radiograph showing the pins that originally held the foil mounts to the maplewood.

mounted on an object with broad shoulders that was capable of standing upright and collapsing in on itself, leaving the 'vandykes' splayed out in the ground. When the drinking-horn complex was lifted, small pieces of wood impressed with the outlines and interlace designs of the smaller panels and 'vandykes' were boxed with the fragments of foil. These were thought to be the remains of the burial chamber roof until radiographs showed that they were pierced by tiny silver nails. The wood was then identified as maple (*acer campestre*), a fine, close-grained honey-coloured wood, and it became clear that the smaller silver-gilt panels and 'vandykes' had decorated maplewood drinking vessels. Amongst the wood were the pieces of one vessel that had been on its side when it was crushed by the collapse of the chamber and this, when assembled, suggested a narrow-mouthed vessel with an upright neck decorated with three rectangular foil panels and

broad sloping shoulders wide enough for the triangular 'vandykes' to lie across. The ends of some of the more complete 'vandykes' were slightly curved and this suggested that the shoulders fell away beneath the ends of the mounts, perhaps into a rounded base although no wood survives to show this. From these clues the reconstruction of the maplewood bottles grew and although they were unique at the time, work on fragments of wood with metal fittings from the princely burial at Taplow showed that in this rich Anglo-Saxon grave too the dead man had been accompanied by maplewood bottles like those found at Sutton Hoo.

The helmet

The helmet posed different problems of reconstruction. It had been restored unhappily with a jutting face mask, a narrow neck-guard which carried the dragon terminal from the back of the crest, a detail that denied the guard any movement, and small ear flaps. It had been pointed out that as a piece of defensive equipment the reconstruction was flawed in that both the sides of the face and the neck behind the ears were totally unprotected from a thrusting blow. Also the helmet, while clearly based on Roman parade helmets, displayed an uneasy compromise between restoration and the practical evidence of the fragmentary remains.

The pieces used in the restoration had been embedded in a plaster matrix and the first problem was to cut them free and clean the fragments of the plaster that had bonded them. When this was completed the helmet was approached like a giant jigsaw and joining fragments were gradually pieced together. The first breakthrough came with the discovery that the crest was complete (it had been extended with plaster on the first restoration) giving the brow-to-nape measurement. Several large joining fragments from the top of the cap and one of its sides provided the ear-to-ear measurement so that the essential proportions of the cap were established. A plaster of Paris base was made to fit these vital fragments and then, using lumps of modelling clay and long insect pins, other fragments were gradually added or located in general terms on the cap if they contained either lengths of the swaged bronze strips that held the decorative tinned-bronze plates to the iron or patches of the tinned-bronze plates themselves. Certain aspects of the helmet reconstruction were self-evident: the inner ends of

87

the eyebrows are attached to a heavy tang (hidden by the gilt-bronze dragon) which rises from the top of the nose and this implied a vertical lie for the face mask. Shaped fragments with bronze binding provided evidence for the shape of the eye-holes and face mask and for the size and proportions of the long ear flaps and wide neck-guard. Also hidden in the corrosion of one of the fragments was a small iron plate that had been riveted to the cap. This was the only evidence of how the ear flaps and neck-guard were attached to the helmet cap, and it would have originally held a short length of leather which acted as a suspension point or hinge. The leather hinges would have given the helmet-wearer considerable freedom of movement for his arms and shoulders and the free-hanging ear flaps could also be drawn up to the face mask, giving the face almost total protection.

The surface of the helmet was covered with panels of tinned-bronze foil that were impressed with decorative motifs – two figural scenes and two filled with animal interlace. None of these survived complete and the designs were pieced together by

86 A group of fragments from the helmet, including the nose and mouth unit, the crest and one of the three gilt-bronze dragon heads, after the dismantling of the first helmet reconstruction.

drawing the tiny fragments of decoration that survived on many of the pieces of iron, and gradually using these, again like pieces of a rather cryptic jigsaw puzzle, to build up the complete designs. The slow process of reconstruction of the two figural scenes was helped by examples of very similar scenes from Swedish helmets, especially the helmet from Valsgärde 7, and from a gold foil disc brooch from Pliezhausen in Germany.

Other equally detailed work led to the reconstruction of the musical instrument as a round-headed lyre similar to other contemporary instruments, to the re-creation of the chainwork with all its decorative virtuosity, which was achieved through radiography of the re-assembled fragments of iron from which it was made, and to a shield reconstruction where the metal and gold foil fittings were mounted on a modern board made of limewood covered with

99

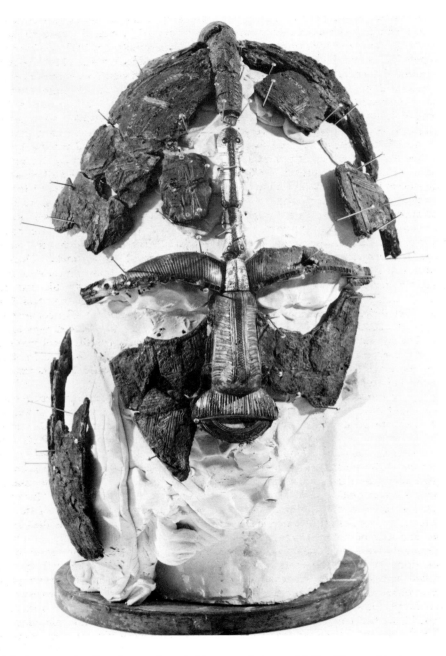

87 The helmet during reconstruction: fragments are held by long pins while their respective positions are considered. Further research showed that the position of the earflaps was too low in relation to the face-mask.

oak-tanned hide. These objects are now highlights of one of the most popular displays in the British Museum, and a lasting tribute to both the painstaking work of the conservators and the background research that provided a firm basis for their restoration.

12 Excavations 1965–70

The results of the 1939 excavations posed the British Museum team several major problems of interpretation apart from the question of grave or cenotaph discussed in chapter 5. How did the ship relate to its trench and the mound that covered it? Did it have a small rounded stern with a re-entrant curve as the published plans suggested? Was it keel-less? Had fragments of some of the objects been overlooked in the excavation and, if so, could they be recovered from the spoil heaps? What was the original shape of the mound? Was it an elongated oval or was it circular as Charles Phillips had suggested? To answer these questions it was decided to mount a further programme of excavation on mound 1 to be preceded by a complete survey of the barrow group.

The objectives of the project were three-fold. The first phase was to record the gravefield in as great detail as possible, by surveying it and producing a contour plan on which a new site plan would be based, and by examining it with the new generation of earth detecting equipment adopted for archaeological use including resistivity and magnetometer surveys. A metal detector survey was also undertaken. The second phase was to re-open the ship-grave, to record the remains of the ship and to determine its relationship to its trench and the mound. The third phase was to excavate and sift the 1939 spoil heaps to recover any tiny fragments of the finds that might have escaped detection in 1939 and then to excavate the mound to determine its structure.

In 1965 the ship-trench was opened and excavation gradually revealed the much damaged structure of the great ship. In three short summer seasons what was left was meticulously recorded: each rivet which remained in position was numbered and labelled with a copper tag and the entire hull was planned at a scale of one inch to the foot – imperial measurements were deliberately used to match the work done in 1939. The casts of the frames that snaked across the hull were also recorded on the rivet plans, as were breaks in the skin of the ship and the positions of the sections that Commander Hutchison had cut across the keel plank and end-posts in 1939. These sections were cut back and drawn in 1967 in an attempt to recapture the cross-sections of the ship's spine. The relationship of the ship to its trench and mound was recorded for the first time and a vertical photomosaic of the hull was made.

At this stage the possibility was considered of preserving the ship in the same way as the Viking long-ship found at Ladby in Denmark which had been covered by a small 'museum' after its excavation. Unfortunately in 1939 the ship impression was not backfilled with the sand that had been taken out of it and which would have preserved it. Instead the magnificent ship was left unprotected except for a thick layer of cut bracken and a few pieces of sacking, and the gunwale and upper strakes gradually crumbled. During the early part of the Second World War the gravefield and the open heath to the east of it were taken over by the army for use as a training area. The partially silted ship-trench and the spoil-clad mound were used for practice manoeuvres, slit trenches were cut across the stern of the ship and the mound was used for mortar practice until the intervention of an archaeologically-minded officer, E.V. Wright, the excavator of the Bronze Age Ferriby boats. Thus the British Museum's excavations revealed a much battered impression whose sandy fill was full of rivets from the upper strakes that had fallen into the hull as the sides of the ship collapsed. Reluctantly it was decided that the hull was too damaged to merit preservation as the focal point of an on-site display and that the impression should be dug through to make sure that nothing was buried beneath it.

Before this drastic and destructive step a permanent three-dimensional record of the remains of the ship was clearly essential and it was decided to make a cast of it in plaster of Paris – curiously this was discussed in 1939 as the best way of preserving the ship, but was rejected on both logistical and financial grounds. During the summer of 1967 conservators from the British Museum tackled the problem of making a mould of the fragile eighty-foot long impression. It was decided to make the mould in interlocking sections, and before applying the plaster the ship was protected by covering each rivet with a 'hat' of modelling clay and then stippling damp sheets of tissue paper onto the surface of the sand. When the cast was complete a block and tackle was rigged from the scaffolding roof, and after numbering, planning and levelling, the sections were lifted and transported to London. In 1968 they were pieced together like a giant jigsaw puzzle from which a fibre-glass positive was made. After the plaster cast was lifted from the ship and each rivet and copper tag had been collected the remains of the ship's skin were removed to reveal natural undisturbed sand throughout the length of the ship-trench.

88 The surface of the ship is prepared for plastering by covering the rivets with modelling clay and placing sheets of damp tissue paper on the sand.

One of the crucial questions that the 1965–7 excavations were designed to answer was whether or not a body had been placed in the burial chamber (as discussed on pages 39–40). In an attempt to resolve this it was decided to measure the level of residual phosphates throughout the ship. The principle behind this is that as bone decays, the phosphate which it contains dissolves into the surrounding soil, where it can be held if the soil itself has been in contact with corroding iron. There was iron throughout the ship in a regular pattern where the rivets had fastened the planking as well as large iron objects in the burial chamber, so that the levels of phosphate could be consistently measured. It was

hoped that a higher level of residual phosphate would be found within the chamber, indicating the presence of a large phosphatic source which could have been the body.

The results of the phosphate survey showed that although only very small levels of residual phosphates survived a difference did exist between the levels inside and outside the burial chamber, which confirmed that there was a major source of phosphate in the grave; unfortunately it is not possible to tell whether the source was human or animal. Later excavations at Sutton Hoo have demonstrated very clearly how skeletal material can vanish almost entirely in the gravefield's acid conditions and the confirmation of this phenomenon from other Anglo-Saxon sites and modern Scandinavian excavations suggests that the interpretation of the ship-grave as an inhumation is the most probable.

89 The excavation of mound 1 (1968), showing the empty ship-trench and the structure of the mound in the vertical section faces.

As the phosphate project drew to a close in August 1967 work began on searching the 1939 spoil heaps for fragments of the objects from the burial chamber and the examination of the Anglo-Saxon mound beneath the heaps. The first season, directed by Paul Ashbee, was devoted to the mantle of spoil that concealed the two surviving lobes of mound 1 and a crescent-shaped dump at the east end of the ship-trench which was the spoil from Basil Brown's initial six-foot trench into the mound. Remarkably few fragments from the principal objects buried in the grave were found. The most important are a tine from the bronze stag, a couple of fragments from the iron of the helmet, a boar's

head escutcheon and a few short lengths of the escutcheon frames from the large Celtic hanging-bowl, a gilt-bronze dragon's head with tiny cabochon garnet eyes from the rim of the shield and a horn from one of the animal heads on the stand. The lack of finds in the spoil heaps is an indication of the enormous care taken in 1939 to recover every fragment of the damaged objects despite the chaotic conditions in the collapsed burial chamber.

Once the spoil heaps had been excavated revealing the surface of the barrow that had been buried in 1939, work began on the excavation and recording of the Anglo-Saxon mound. It was decided to excavate the barrow to the buried Anglo-Saxon ground surface, to record any features in it and to sample it for pollen analysis, and then to strip the area down to the natural sand to see whether the mound had been surrounded by a ditch or whether any traces remained of the system used to lower the great ship into its grave. It had been suggested, for example, that the ship might have been pushed out over the trench on rollers before being lowered into it and that ropes wrapped around bollards driven deeply into the sand could have been used in the final stages to manoeuvre the ship into the tightly-fitting trench.

One of the objectives of the mound excavation was to establish its original shape as it was uncertain whether it had been more or less circular or an elongated oval to cover the exceptionally long ship, and also to achieve an estimate of its height before the destruction of the central area by the 1939 excavations. The structure of the barrow was also of great interest as no Anglo-Saxon burial mound had been excavated using modern archaeological techniques.

Excavations showed that the construction of the mound had been carefully organised. First the soil and subsoil over the area where the ship-trench was to be dug had been removed and stored for back-filling. Then a trench only a little larger than the ship was carefully dug and the clean yellow sand from it was dumped in two distinct areas to either side. After the ship was lowered into the tight-fitting trench the soil and subsoil may have been used to fill the ship, but the clean yellow sand to either side of the trench was left – perhaps as a marker for the mound builders. The mound itself was made largely of sandy soil and subsoil which must have been collected from a large deturfed area

nearby; it was built with an average diameter of just under 30 m and a height that must have been at least 3 m (the estimated height in 1939). The earth barrow was furnished with a capping of turf. It was not surrounded by a ditch.

The stripping of the mound to reveal the buried ground surface did not uncover any evidence that could be related to the time of the burial. However examination of the buried Anglo-Saxon soil horizons revealed a series of parallel striations – perhaps the result of pre-barrow ploughing – and pollen analyses from the buried soil containing a high percentage of grass and cereal pollens showed that the barrow was built on land that had been cultivated.

The final phase of the British Museum's excavations at Sutton Hoo was an investigation in 1969 of a small area of the more or less flat land between mound 1 and mound 12 which led in the following year to the excavation of the south-east quadrant of mound 5. These excavations produced some of the most surprising results of the 1965–70 seasons by uncovering a combination of prehistoric palisade trenches and Anglo-Saxon burials that indicated a complex stratigraphical development of the site over a couple of thousand years or more. In 1969 the excavations, directed by Dr Ian Longworth from the British Museum, uncovered part of a straight-sided

90 North-south and east-west sections through the ship-burial based on information from the 1965–9 excavations, showing the height and spread of the mound and its relation to the ship-trench.

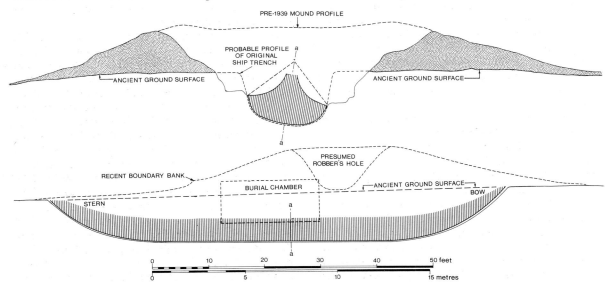

91 Large oval pit with a skull buried at its eastern end. Only the teeth, two vertebrae and fragments of the heavier facial bones survived. The shape of the skull remained as crusted sand that crumbled when it was lifted.

palisade ditch, part of an enclosure that dates from the middle Neolithic. This was traced across the site in the following year in a series of small trenches as far as the limits of the scheduled area. Little evidence for the date of the palisade trench was recovered, and it is not clear for what purpose it was dug – whether it was part of an enclosure for animals, or perhaps for a settlement. However in the context of the prehistoric ditches and pits found by Ashbee beneath mound 1, the Bronze Age Beaker material that Basil Brown records from his excavations in 1938 and 1939, and the small quantity of Iron Age material that was recovered during Longworth's excavations and the digging of a silage pit immediately to the west of the scheduled area in the 1950s, it became clear the the area surrounding the Anglo-Saxon cemetery had been in continual, even if seasonal, use from the Neolithic until the Iron Age.

Longworth's excavations also uncovered an unexpected range of Anglo-Saxon burials. In the area that impinged on the southern flank of mound 5, two unaccompanied inhumations and the remains of a third were uncovered. These were apparently not placed in coffins and were buried with no personal possessions, so there is no indication of their status or their date of burial. In the small area opened between mounds 1 and 12 a large oval pit aligned on an east/west axis was uncovered. This contained nothing but the crusted outline, teeth and occasional bones of a skull that had been buried

while still articulated with the two top vertebrae. Fragments of bone from the skull have been dated by radio-carbon analysis to 1204 ± 79 BP ($c.$ AD 740). The skull lay close to the eastern end of the pit, and close by on the edge of the pit, high up in the fill, was a crushed fragment of bronze sheeting with repoussé decoration in a confused animal style, perhaps part of a decorative mount from an early seventh-century small bucket. To the east of the oval skull pit a heap of cremated bone was found, as well as an undecorated cremation urn of late sixth- or early seventh-century date that contained the remains of a young man.

For the first time at Sutton Hoo Longworth's excavations produced the phenomenon of the organic crusting of human tissue – a phenomenon 92 that was familiar to archaeologists who had worked on the ship between 1965 and 1967 from the curious way in which the sand had replaced the organic structure of the wood so that the square-cut frames, for example, survived as square-shaped casts with a crusted surface. Essentially the process (which is currently being studied as part of the contemporary Sutton Hoo project) seems to be that as organic matter decays it is replaced by sand so that the original surface contours survive as a distinct and fairly hard sandy carapace that allows the skilled excavator of, for example, an inhumation, to follow the outlines of the original fully-fleshed body. The relative fragility of the body shapes makes it very clear that it would not have been possible for the

92 One of the first sand-bodies excavated at Sutton Hoo during the 1970 excavations.

excavators in 1939 to have recovered a similar shape in the collapsed burial chamber. In any case the body would probably have disintegrated before the chamber fell in so that only decaying skeletal material would have been finally enveloped in the sand.

Although Longworth's excavations were necessarily limited in scale the evidence he recovered for the prehistoric use of the site and of the different styles of Anglo-Saxon burials between the mounds pointed to a longer and more detailed historical sequence than had been supposed. It was partly to unravel this sequence that a totally new archaeological project was begun in 1983.

13 The kingdom of East Anglia

Almost nothing is known of the history of the kingdom of the East Angles in the formative years during the sixth and early seventh century. The two principal sources are the *Anglo-Saxon Chronicle* and the *Historia Ecclesiastica* which was written by the historian Bede in the early eighth century. The first mention of the kingdom in the *Anglo-Saxon Chronicle* is an entry for the year 617 which tells us that Aethelfrith, king of Northumbria, was killed by Raedwald, king of the East Angles. Bede's first reference is contained in a brief account of the death of Aethelbert of Kent who died in 616 and was succeeded as the overlord of the English kings by Raedwald. According to Bede, Raedwald 'even while Aethelbert was alive had been obtaining the leadership of his own race'.

Thus there are no written sources for the earlier period when the Sutton Hoo cemetery may have been established as a royal burial place and no information on the consolidation of the kingdom after settlement by people of Germanic origin in the fifth century. It is in fact even difficult at this period to define what territories constituted the kingdom of the East Angles although its core was the modern counties of Suffolk and Norfolk. From the mid-sixth century the East Angles were ruled by the Wuffinga dynasty whose names are given in an early eighth-century East Anglian king-list (BL Cotton Vespasian BVI fol. 109v) which characteristically traces the dynasty's descent through Woden (see page 122). A gloss in *Historia Brittonum*, written by Geoffrey of Monmouth, describes Wehha, the father of Wuffa who gave his name to the East Anglian dynasty, as being the first to rule over the people of East Anglia. This sparse information suggests that by the mid-sixth century, or a little before, the territories of the East Angles, settled by incomers from the other side of the North Sea, had coalesced into a kingdom. But what was that kingdom like, and how did Sutton Hoo fit into it?

These, unfortunately, are questions that are more or less impossible to answer. Geographically Sutton Hoo is isolated from the large cremation cemeteries of Cambridgeshire and Norfolk where archaeology suggests the most dense pattern of settlement developed. But it was strategically placed for easy access to the sea and this may have played a part in its siting. At the time when mound 1 was built, the land surrounding the cemetery was open and the mounds would have been clearly visible from the river, and from the other side of the river where the land is lower than the plateau on whose edge the

gravefield lies. But the area around Sutton Hoo may perhaps have had a special significance for the Wuffingas. Bede, writing of the conversion of the East Saxon king Swithhelm in the mid-seventh century, says that his baptism took place at Rendlesham, four miles up the Deben from Sutton Hoo, which he describes as a *vicus regius* – a royal residence. A little further north, close to the river Alde, is Snape, the site of a mixed cemetery which contains the only other Anglo-Saxon ship-burial beneath a mound other than those at Sutton Hoo. This concentration of a royal residence and two unusual cemeteries cannot be wholly coincidental, and if the specific East Swedish elements in the Sutton Hoo ship-burial are seen in relation to the geographical isolation of Snape, Rendlesham and Sutton Hoo on the Suffolk sandlings, it becomes possible to link the three sites with the arrival of a group of Swedish incomers (perhaps from the Uppland area where Sutton Hoo's closest links lie in the chieftains' graves of Vendel and Valsgärde) who settled in a landscape that was not entirely unlike their homeland.

If the genealogical tables can be relied on, only four generations lie between Wehha, the first king of East Anglia, and Raedwald, who succeeded on the death of Tyttla in about 599 and who took over the mantle of Aethelbert on his death in 616 when he became the fifth holder of what Bede describes as the *imperium*, a form of overlordship that made him chief amongst the English kings. In these four generations there must have been a dynamic consolidation of the political strength of the East Anglian kingdom and a rapidly increasing wealth that made possible the commission of the magnificent gold and garnet jewellery buried in mound 1. But not a trace of this development survives, although it is possible to catch glimpses from brief passages in *Historia Ecclesiastica* of the continual interaction between the courts of the heptarchy and the political manoeuvering and tactical skirmishing that was an integral part of English life in the late sixth and early seventh century.

Raedwald was converted to Christianity while on a visit to the court of Aethelbert of Kent, but according to Bede, he quickly reverted to paganism when he returned to his own kingdom. After his death in 624 or 625 the kingdom was ruled first by his son Eorpwald, of whom it is known only that he was converted to Christianity and is thought to have been killed shortly afterwards, when the kingdom 'fell into error' for several years. In 631/2

Sigeberht, Eorpwald's half-brother who had taken refuge in France during Raedwald's reign, returned to England to rule. He was a devout Christian, so devout that after a few years governing the still largely pagan East Anglians and fostering the cause of Christianity he handed over the reins of power to Ecric, his kinsman, so that he could return to monastic life. Ecric, about whom nothing is known, ruled alone until the threat to East Anglian sovereignty from Mercia grew so great that Sigeberht was persuaded to leave his monastery to lead the East Anglians against Penda. According to Bede he went into battle armed only with a wooden staff. Both he and Ecric were killed fighting the Mercians, and Anna, a Christian, succeeded to the kingdom and ruled until his death in 653.

During Sigeberht's short reign Christianity began to take a firmer hold in East Anglia. According to Bede the king was eager to see his kingdom adopt the Christian religion and this led to a mission by Bishop Felix who lived and worked for seventeen years at Dunwich, where he founded an episcopal see. Also during Sigeberht's reign, Fursa, an Irish monk, preached in the kingdom and converted many of the East Angles; he eventually built a monastery on ground granted to him by Sigeberht which was possibly situated at Burgh Castle.

The few historical windows that exist provide a shadowy impression of the gradual emergence of the kingdom of the East Angles and the wheeling and dealing of the ruling clan, but the relationship between the king, his court and his subjects is difficult to define. Too little is known about communication, organisation or codes of behaviour in this early period to enable any form of relationship to be analysed. Thus the gravefield at Sutton Hoo, set aside from the mainstream of contemporary life in East Anglia by its royal burial, may never be fully integrated in the history of the kingdom of the East Angles – unless some day it can be associated with the so far undiscovered settlement that must have developed alongside it.

14 Dating the ship burial

The date of the burial

The wealth and style of the Sutton Hoo ship-burial immediately suggested that it was a royal grave probably belonging to one of the seventh-century East Anglian kings, yet the identity of the dead man, which depended on the date of the burial, proved elusive. This was because the purse full of coins which had been buried with him belonged to 77, 78 the currency of Merovingian Gaul whose chronology was extremely complex. The coins, of course, cannot date the burial itself, but obviously the date of the latest coins would give archaeologists an indication of the earliest date that they could have been buried. The coins cannot be used alone as an indication of date, because, like the Anastasius dish (made between 498 and 516), they could well have been kept in a royal treasury for a considerable length of time after their assembly. The coins must therefore be used together with other evidence of period – the art-styles decorating the metalwork, for example – and the pagan style of the burial itself must be related to the known historical and religious background of the kingdom. It is difficult to imagine that a king of an East Anglia which had adopted Christianity with its austere style of burial would have been buried in so arrogantly pagan a manner.

In the years following the excavation the estimated date for the coin collection suggested that the burial must have taken place in the second half of the seventh century, between 650 and 660, a date that was in conflict with both the decorative style of the metalwork and the religious beliefs in a Christian East Anglia. In 1960 however the chronology of the Merovingian coinage, on which the date of the Sutton Hoo coins depended, was drastically revised and a date around 625 was suggested for the latest coins in the Sutton Hoo grave. As an integral part of the research for the publication of the Sutton Hoo find it was decided to attempt an independent dating for the collection using a simple technique to calculate the gold content of a large sample of Merovingian coins – including those from Sutton Hoo. It was known that during the hundred years between 575 and 675 the Merovingian gold coinage was gradually debased and it was thought that if the gold content of a wide range of known-date Merovingian tremisses (inscribed with the name of a king, for example) was measured they could provide a comparative framework into which the Sutton Hoo coins could be fitted. The gold content of over seven hundred tremisses was calculated and a chronology was established which confirmed that the latest coins in the Sutton Hoo purse could be dated to around 625, coincidentally the date of the death of one of East Anglia's greatest kings, Raedwald.

The coins seem to form a deliberate collection rather than a random group selected for burial from the royal treasury, and if so they may have come as a group into East Anglia from Merovingian Gaul – perhaps as a diplomatic present to the king or even as a funerary gift – a gift from the living to the dead. If the date of the latest coin is c.625 clearly a little time must be allowed for the group to have been assembled and sent to England, but however they came into East Anglia and whatever the motive behind their collection, they are vital because they narrow the quest for the identity of the dead man.

As we have seen in chapter 13 East Anglia was ruled between 625 and 636/7 by at least four men: Raedwald, Eorpwald, Sigeberht and Ecric. The burial could belong to any one of these but the grandeur of the grave-goods points to a long and successful reign rather than a brief and inglorious one. It seems reasonable therefore to eliminate both Eorpwald and Ecric on these grounds. Sigeberht had strong connections with Merovingian Gaul, which is argued may account for some of the Merovingian influences in the grave, but if Bede is correct in his description of Sigeberht's devout Christian beliefs it would surely have been more appropriate for his equally devout successor, Anna, to have given his kinsman a Christian burial, perhaps in the monastery that Sigeberht left to confront the Mercians.

In a sense, the identity of the dead king can also only be seen against the finds that accompanied him, and some of the grave's most spectacular objects – the gold and garnet jewellery, and especially the shoulder-clasps and the purse-lid – have a homogeneity that suggests the work of a master craftsman working to a personal royal commission. The dead man is shown by his possessions to have been both a warrior and a ruler who was able to command the production of major works of art for his regalia, but while the purse-lid and gold buckle are magnificent examples of fashionable types the shoulder-clasps are extraordinary in a seventh-century context, taken as they are directly from the parade gear of a Roman legionary. Could they be a reflection of an unusual status – a status that is perhaps echoed by the stag-crowned whetstone that has been interpreted as a sceptre and a symbol of the personal temporal authority of the dead man? If the interpretation of these unique finds is correct then the dead man, apart from being a successful ruler, may have held some special rank, and this is true of Raedwald who for the last eight years of his life was high king among the English. Although the date of Raedwald's death in 624/5 is uncomfortably near the date of the minting of the later coins in the purse, there is little doubt that he alone has the attributes that would make him the most suitable ruler to have been buried in the ship-grave. He had a long successful reign and he was clearly a politically astute ruler, negotiating for the

imperium, as Bede dryly points out, even during the lifetime of its fourth holder, Aethelbert of Kent. His wealth and status and his twenty-five-year reign would have given him the means, the impetus and the time to commission the gold and garnet regalia, yet the problem remains that the date of his death is too close to the estimated date of the latest coins for it to be certain that the ship-burial is his grave. With no historic sources to affirm the identity of the buried king it is only possible to suggest that the most suitable candidate is Raedwald, but to keep an open mind about the other three rulers of East Anglia – Sigeberht, Ecric and Eorpwald.

15 Sutton Hoo: poetry and style

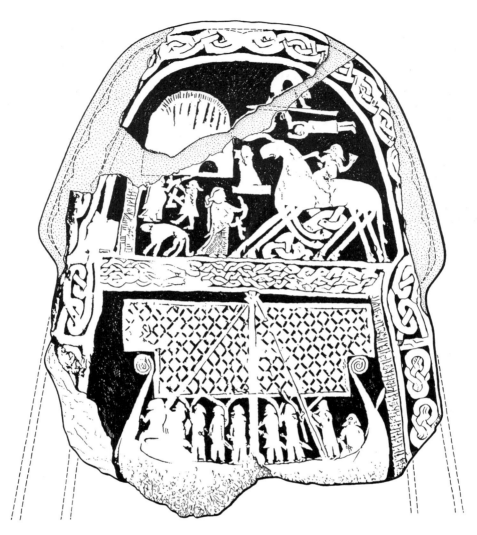

The discovery of a royal grave at Sutton Hoo, packed with a magnificent range of possessions, had a startling effect on the interpretation of Anglo-Saxon culture. Although princely burials of much the same date had been excavated in the nineteenth century at Snape and Taplow, many archaeologists maintained the belief that after the Romans left northern Europe the material culture of the barbarians plummeted. The Anglo-Saxons were generally visualised as living in small, sunken-floored, smoke-laden huts in a state of squalor and poverty (although it was known that in Kent at least they had buried their dead with exquisite metalwork). Nothing could have been further from the kind of life depicted in the poem *Beowulf*, written in Old English in the first half of the eighth century but

93 Scene from an eighth-century picture stone from Tjängvide in Gotland, Sweden, showing Sleipnir, Odin's eight-legged horse, perhaps carrying Odin himself, and a welcoming Valkyrie. The building in the background may be a stylised representation of Valhalla. The scene is an illustration of the Swedish concept of the afterlife, where warriors who die in battle are carried off to feast in Odin's halls.

describing events surrounding two Scandinavian tribes, the Danes of Zealand and the Geats of south Sweden, that had taken place about two hundred years earlier.

In the poem the highest ranks of society are described as living in high-roofed, wide gabled halls, drinking beer and mead to the sound of the harp and the minstrel's voice. The warriors are armed with broad, gold-covered shields, fine swords and spears and wear visored helmets decorated with boar images and mail shirts whose links sing as the men march. Such images as these were regarded as poetic embellishment, as were the descriptions in the poem of the ship-burial of Scyld (one of the Danish kings) and the burial beneath a high mound of Beowulf, the hero of the poem who was killed as he fought with a dragon guarding an immense hoard of treasure also buried beneath a mound. Sutton Hoo quite suddenly revealed that such a heroic way of life was not beyond the realms of probability in sixth- and seventh-century East Anglia.

It was not merely the magnificent gold and garnet jewellery, or the helmet, shield and sword that fleshed out the Beowulf poem, but objects like the ornate suspension chain and its large cauldron (which between them would have needed a cross-beam height of at least 5 m to hang, implying a roof height of perhaps as much as 7 m) and the heavy textiles that survived only as scraps throughout the chamber and which are interpreted as floor coverings or hangings. To judge from his domestic possessions the East Anglian king lived in no bare hovel. The excavation of a Northumbrian royal hall at Yeavering that was over 25 m long has also given the archaeologist a detailed ground-plan of a building built with massive timbers which, if placed in an East Anglian context, could be easily reconstructed into suitable surroundings for the Sutton Hoo chain and cauldron; a hall in which the elegant drinking horns and maplewood bottles, the hanging-bowls, gaming-pieces and the lyre would not have appeared out of place.

But the finds also give us some idea of the way in which an early seventh-century ruler took stock of his status – he was buried not only with equipment representing his prowess as a warrior (helmet, shield and sword, spear, mail shirt and two-handed axe) but with a group of possessions which make a deliberate statement of authority: the shoulder-clasps, the sceptre and the stand. If the burial is indeed that of Raedwald and these unique objects are the individual trappings of the high king (holder of the *imperium*) then as a deliberate display of the symbols of power so familiar in the Roman Empire, it may suggest a classical ancestry to the *imperium* which we cannot now define.

The burial, together with the ship-burial at Snape and the burial beneath a substantial mound at Taplow, also gives a ring of truth to the accounts of the burials of both Scyld and Beowulf that are re-counted in detail in the poem. Scyld is described as being pushed out to sea in an ice-covered ship that was ready to sail. Although this abandoning to the waves of the dead king and his treasures seems to suggest a form of burial very different from the ship-burial at Sutton Hoo, it may be that the description of the ship as ice-covered simply suggests that Scyld died in the deepest part of winter when the ground would have been too hard to dig a ship-sized grave. Whatever the interpretation of the style of burial, the poem makes clear that Scyld was accompanied by 'a great store of treasure, wealth from lands far away'. (Quotations from E. Talbot Donaldson's prose translation of *Beowulf*.) His ship 'was furnished with iron-weapons and battle-dress, swords and mail-shirts' and 'on his breast lay a great many treasures that should voyage with him far out into the sea's possession ... Then also they set a gold standard high over his head.' The similarities between the form of burial and the choice of contents between Sutton Hoo and the funeral of Scyld is remarkable.

Beowulf, in contrast, was cremated and his funeral pyre was 'hung with helmets, battle-shields, bright mail shirts'. After the cremation his people, the Geats, 'built a mound on a promontory, one that was high and broad, widely seen by sea-farers, and in ten days completed a monument for the bold in battle [Beowulf], surrounded the remains of the fire with a wall, the most splendid that men most skilled might devise. In the barrow they placed rings and jewels ... They let the earth hold the wealth of the earls, gold in the ground, where now it still dwells, as useless to men as it was before. Then the brave in battle rode round the mound, children of nobles, twelve in all, would bewail their sorrow and mourn their king, recite dirges and speak of the man. They praised his great deeds and his acts of courage, judged well his prowess. So it is fitting that man honour his liege lord with work, love him in heart when he must be led forth from the body. Thus the people of the Geats ... lamented the death of their lord.'

In the styles of both these burials we see elements of the Sutton Hoo ship-burial, and differences. The closest parallel is perhaps the burial of Beowulf (despite the fact that he was cremated) not merely in the contents placed in his grave or cremated with him, but in the deliberate siting of the barrow on a headland, clearly visible from the sea – a striking similarity to the siting of the Sutton Hoo cemetery on the edge of a plateau overlooking the river

Deben. The description of Beowulf's funeral also gives us a little information about the ceremonies that must always have surrounded high-status burials: warriors ride around the mound, dirges are recited and the valiant deeds of the dead man are declaimed. The poet also says that it took ten days to build Beowulf's mound – a complex one with a stone interior. At Sutton Hoo similar ceremonies must have taken place. We know from excavations that the digging of the ship-trench and the building of the barrow were carefully organised, and the hauling of the great ship up from the river overland, for perhaps as much as a mile if a gradual approach to the cemetery was chosen, must have involved men from the entire community. All the preparations must have been undertaken with the solemn ceremony that Beowulf suggests.

It is fascinating to speculate on contemporary attitudes towards death and the afterlife but our knowledge of pagan beliefs in this early period is almost non-existent. It is thought that goods were buried or cremated to ensure that they went with their owner to the next world, which in Scandinavian mythology is described as Valhalla, the hall

93

where warriors feast with Odin. It was not only warrior equipment or fine jewellery that was thought to be needed in the afterlife but simple domestic equipment like tubs and buckets. Food, too, was often placed in a grave. The strength of pagan belief must have been sufficient to prevent the robbing of graves like Sutton Hoo in the lifetime of those who took part in the burial. The ritual differences between inhumation and cremation are hard to understand, but to those concerned such magnificent objects were in either case, as the Beowulf poet reminds us, 'useless to men'.

The story of Beowulf describes a Scandinavian setting that is brought to life by Sutton Hoo but there are also cultural strands in the ship-burial itself that suggest a Scandinavian ancestry for the dynasty that ruled East Anglia. Swedish influences have always been recognised in some of the sinuous art styles which decorated English metalwork in the sixth and seventh centuries, but in East Anglia the

94 Map showing the relationship of Sutton Hoo to the cemeteries of Vendel and Valsgärde and other find-spots mentioned in the text.

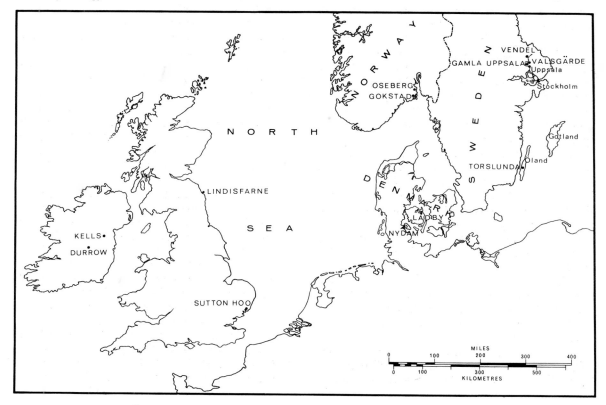

link is more specific. When the burial was excavated, some of the principal objects – the helmet, the shield and even the drinking horns – were claimed as Swedish and immediately compared with the finds from the chieftains' graves of Vendel and Valsgärde in the Uppland region north of Stockholm, as well as the royal grave of Old Uppsala, where a cloisonné pyramid and fragment of silver foil impressed with a dancing warrior scene are remarkably similar to those of Sutton Hoo. At Old Uppsala the king and his possessions had been cremated before being placed beneath an exceptionally large mound in a way that is almost a direct reflection of the funeral of Beowulf. In contrast, at both Vendel and Valsgärde, the members of the chieftains' families were buried with their possessions in clinker-built boats, and the Valsgärde cemetery lay on a ridge overlooking the river Fyris in a situation very much like the Sutton Hoo and Snape cemeteries.

Although there are striking similarities of custom between the ship-burial at Sutton Hoo and those of Vendel and Valsgärde, there are also interesting and significant differences. In the Swedish graves for example, the chieftains in some cases are buried with more than one shield or sword; perhaps the arms of retainers were placed in the grave to accompany the dead man, as was maybe the case at Taplow (where current research shows that three shield bosses were placed in the grave). The Swedish graves also differ in that the chieftains' dogs, horses, and even hunting birds were buried together with their harnesses and bridles which were decorated with elegantly designed mounts. At Sutton Hoo, similar decorative mounts would have survived even if all the animal bones had leached away in the acid soil. Nothing was found in mound 1 (though among the cremated bone in both mounds 3 and 4 fragments of a horse and dog survived). Despite such important differences of ritual between the Swedish and the Sutton Hoo burials, there must be a direct cultural connection, as archaeology suggests that the practice of high-status boat-burial in the sixth and early seventh century is restricted to just one small area of Sweden and an equally small area of East Anglia.

The most startling similarities between East Anglia and Sweden occur in the contents of the Sutton Hoo burial. The helmet and the shield are both so like the Swedish helmets and shields that at first glance it seems impossible that they were not made alongside them (although differences in con-

struction suggest that the helmet at least is the product of an English workshop). Iconographically the helmet is most closely related to the Valsgärde 7 helmet which shares both the fallen warrior and the dancing warrior scenes, while the shield finds its closest comparison in one of the magnificent shields from the Vendel XII burial where the boss and the interlace motifs on the foil strips are so close to those decorating the Sutton Hoo shield that they have been attributed to the same workshop, if not the same craftsman.

There are other stylistic details that show immediate Swedish influence in, for example, the single animal that fills one of the panels on the dragon from the front of the shield, or in the predatory bird that lies across the shield board. But although these designs are indisputably Swedish, does it imply that the shield and helmet were actually made in Sweden and brought to England? Is it possible to distinguish between an object actually made in a Swedish workshop, and one made by Swedish craftsmen working in an English milieu? It can be said immediately that nothing has yet been excavated in Sweden that rivals the quality of the shield fittings or their elegant designs, but it is also true that an equivalent royal inhumation has not been excavated – the two exceptionally rich graves of Old Uppsala and Huseby Långhundra were both cremations and only scraps of metalwork survived. Occasional finds of fine metalwork – the gold and garnet sword pommels from Hög Edsten or Vallstenarum for example, the former so like the Sutton Hoo pommel that they too have been attributed to the same workshop – need not argue a Swedish origin. They could all equally well have been made in Frankish workshops and imported into both Sweden and England.

If anything throws doubt on the Swedish manufacture of the helmet (and perhaps the shield) it is the way that it was made. The helmet cap is formed from a single iron sheet, hammered into shape and then decorated with silvery bronze plates. It has solid iron ear-flaps and neck-guard. The Swedish helmet caps are made from either sections of iron riveted together or a light lattice of iron strips to which the decorative bronze plates were attached. They also have a light flexible system of protection for the face and neck. These fundamental differences suggest a separate manufacturing background to the helmets even if the surface decoration is astonishingly alike, and it seems that the Sutton Hoo helmet is the product of an English smithing

96

95 The shield boss from Vendel XII, very similar to the Sutton Hoo shield boss (fig. 32). The Sutton Hoo boss may have been made in the same Swedish workshop or in East Anglia by Swedish armourers.

tradition but decorated in a Swedish style. The shield is less definable: it is true that its board is made of lime (the wood of Beowulf's shield) whereas most of the Swedish shields are made of pine, but the boss and gold foil strips at least must either have been made in Sweden – and in the same workshops that produced the Vendel XII shield – or by a metalsmith who had come to England from that workshop.

The decoration of the helmet and the shield suggests a mobility amongst top craftsmen, travelling either with their patrons or perhaps independently of them, to fulfil specific commissions, in the same way that stonemasons working on ecclesiastical buildings are known to have done. The metalworkers probably carried with them their tools and dies for stamping bronze foil, like the two bearing simple ribbon interlace patterns which were

found near Bury St Edmunds or the dies probably used for helmet plates that were found at Torslunda, on the Swedish island of Öland. These carry 97 remarkable figural scenes, including a man with a monster's head, an image that seems to be part of a common pool of Germanic and Scandinavian legend whose meaning is beyond our understanding, although it may belong to the same mythological background as the man and monster theme that pervades the poem *Beowulf*.

Fashion then, as now, was a powerful influence and some of the other principal objects in the ship-burial reflect this. The great gold buckle, for example, decorated with interlace, is related to a group of large and extremely rich buckles that in England are found principally in Kent (although the gold buckle from the princely burial at Taplow is perhaps closest to it in terms of sheer wealth) and the equally large iron buckles with silver inlay that are found across the English Channel in Merovingian Gaul. Other objects in the burial, the purse-lid, the sword-pommel, the pyramids and the scabbard

96 One of the Swedish helmets from Valsgärde 5, illustrating very well the superficial resemblance between the Vendel and Valsgärde helmets and the Sutton Hoo helmet (fig. 17). Note the elegant cast bronze eyebrows and the iron strips that protect the neck.

slider for example, are all familiar to the archaeologist from a variety of European contexts. At Sutton Hoo, the current styles are followed but at a supremely high level in that they are made of gold and superbly decorated with cloisonné garnets. Even the storage vessels, the tub, buckets and the two smaller cauldrons, belong to common types, while the drinking horns and maplewood bottles share their style of rich fittings with those from the Taplow burial, although the motifs used to decorate them are different. Finally the lyre is clearly typical of its time, closely matched by one, again from Taplow, and two others from Cologne in Germany.

At Sutton Hoo there are unique objects – the sceptre, the stand and the shoulder-clasps – and these, it has been argued, were placed in the grave to represent the particular status of the man buried in it, but most of the other finds are exceptional only because of their richness. Sutton Hoo reflects the melange of fashionable styles that were current in late sixth- and early seventh-century Europe (from the Rhine to the Atlantic coast) and Sweden. There are no signs of artistic innovation in the metalwork: the metalsmith who made the great gold buckle or the purse-lid was clearly a supreme craftsman but he worked within well-defined paths, using a repertoire of familiar themes that are made special because of his own particular genius; it is his brilliance that lifts the finest objects of the Sutton Hoo ship-burial into a class of their own.

97 Two of four heavy bronze dies, found at Torslunda in
Öland, Sweden, used to stamp decorative foils and
possibly to decorate helmets like that of Sutton Hoo. One
shows a lively portrayal of a man between two bear-like
beasts, similar to the scene on the Sutton Hoo purse-lid;
the other a helmeted warrior fleeing a wolf-headed figure.

16 Sutton Hoo today

The excavations at Sutton Hoo 1 between 1965 and 1970 answered a number of questions about the great ship-burial, but problems of interpretation have always dogged the archaeologists' understanding of the gravefield as a whole. The existence of mound 5 was established, although it was barely visible on the ground, but did this imply that there were other equally low mounds that had not been identified? The discovery of isolated unaccompanied inhumations and cremations seemed to bring Sutton Hoo into line with the mixed burial practices seen for example at Snape, but also made it clear that the area of the cemetery was not necessarily defined by the extent of the mounds. What, then, were the limits of the Anglo-Saxon gravefield and how did it grow? How long was it in use and when did it begin? Although four mounds had been excavated – three of them lying close together (mounds 1, 3 and 4) – no archaeological evidence for their chronological relationship had been recovered. The use of a single die to decorate the triangular silver-gilt mounts from the drinking horns in both mounds 1 and 2 implies a broad contemporaneity between two of the mounds, but what of the chronology of the rest? Could some sequence of mound construction be determined from fresh excavation? Evidence also abounded at Sutton Hoo for the use of the site from the middle Neolithic until the later phases of the Iron Age, and the occasional flint tools, hearths and a few fragments of Bronze Age clay loom-weights suggested the likelihood of some form of settlement near or on the site. Could the relationship of the cemetery to the underlying prehistoric landscape be defined? Equally could its relationship to the kingdom of the East Angles be more clearly understood through renewed fieldwork and research?

In an attempt to answer some of these questions and to place the gravefield in its wider historical context a new project of excavation and research was launched in 1983 by the specially created Sutton Hoo Research Trust, directed by Martin Carver of the University of York. The project was supported by the British Museum, the Society of Antiquaries of

98 Summer 1991: the excavated sample, looking east. Mound 1 is in the bottom right-hand corner.

London, the British Broadcasting Corporation and the National Maritime Museum and was carried out in close collaboration with the Suffolk Archaeological Unit. The first phase of the field project was an intensive programme of pre-excavation survey designed to re-examine the scheduled area and its immediate surroundings with the most modern electronic equipment, including a soil-sounding radar, modifying a system that had originally been developed to detect changes in the composition of the Polar ice-caps. It was hoped that this would be able to detect anomalies beneath the spongy turf smaller than ditches, for example, which responded to other methods of remote sensing (magnetometer survey, resistivity survey). A new contour survey, using an electronic distance measurer, was made of the mounds and the land around them and a programme of field-walking was begun to recover surface finds in the vicinity of the gravefield.

The programme evaluation continued with the excavation of long trenches on the east, south and west borders of the cemetery in order to discover its limits. Within the scheduled area, an anti-glider ditch, one of many that form a lattice of ditches cut across the flat open countryside near Sutton Hoo in anticipation of a German airborne invasion during World War 2, was excavated to examine a section across one of the flat areas of the site. This produced little of relevance to the history of the gravefield but amply demonstrated how the roots of the dense bracken cover had destroyed the coherence of the thin archaeological layer between the ground surface and the natural sand. Another intervention examined Basil Brown's 1938 trench through mound 2 – the mound that contained the ransacked remains of a small boat. The object of this was to examine the remains of the inside of an Anglo-Saxon barrow and to establish exactly what Basil Brown had excavated in 1938, whether it was a boat or a ransacked boat trench.

The long trenches running out into the agricultural land to the east and south of the site, and in the woodland to the west, were designed to trace the extent of the archaeological zone beyond the scheduled area. A fourth trench, cut into the eastern edge of a silage pit dug in the 1950s where sherds of Iron Age pottery were found, was also opened. All the trenches, with the exception of the one in the sloping woodland to the west of the site, produced evidence of extensive prehistoric activity close to the site but diminishing within the limits of the trenches. The Neolithic, Bronze Age and Iron Age were all well represented in terms of abraded potsherds, flint as-

semblages, occasional groups of postholes, working surfaces, hearths and ditches. No evidence of activity on the site during the Roman occupation was recovered, reflecting the results of Longworth's excavations in 1969/70, and what happened to the site during this period remains an area of speculation.

In 1986 the evaluation was completed, and a six-year programme of excavation began, revealing more than 1 hectare of the Anglo-Saxon cemetery. At the eastern edge was a group of eighteen inhumations, of which ten unexpectedly showed clear signs of ritual trauma. A second group, including seven showing ritual trauma, was later found to encircle Mound 5. The 'sand-bodies', as they were quickly christened, are similar in every way to those excavated in 1969 and 1970. They show a variety of different forms – one was buried in a semi-crouched position, another, beheaded, lay stretched out with the head placed in the crook of his arm, another lay in a half upright position almost as though sitting up in the grave. Yet another lay face down with one arm forced up over the back as though the body had been thrown into the grave. A body excavated in 1985 lay as though running, one arm stretched out, apparently holding a piece of wood, perhaps a club or even part of a plough. Radiocarbon dating of organic material from the first group of graves has produced dates from both the seventh and eighth centuries which suggests that the gravefield may have held some significance for some generations after royal burial ceased with the adoption of Christianity in the kingdom of East Anglia in the second quarter of the seventh century.

During the Trust's campaign seven mounds were excavated, mounds 2, 5, 6, 7, 14, 17, and 18. Of these, all but one were found to have been gutted by previous investigations, which, apart from a terse entry in the *Ipswich Journal* in 1860, have left no trace in the archaeological or antiquarian record. The funerary rites recorded from these mounds fall into 92 two groups – cremations beneath mounds 5, 6, 7 and 18 and complex inhumations beneath mounds 2, 14 (a female grave) and 17. The cremation burial rite is 99 repeated in each mound, with the burnt bones and possessions placed inside a copper-alloy bowl, which was then either wrapped or merely covered with textile. The inhumations, although largely destroyed, all have different styles of burial. Mound 2 was originally interpreted as a boat burial, with the boat in a pit below ground level, but its re-excavation showed that what Basil Brown had interpreted as a small, transom-sterned boat was in fact the interior of a robber trench, beneath which lay the trampled and

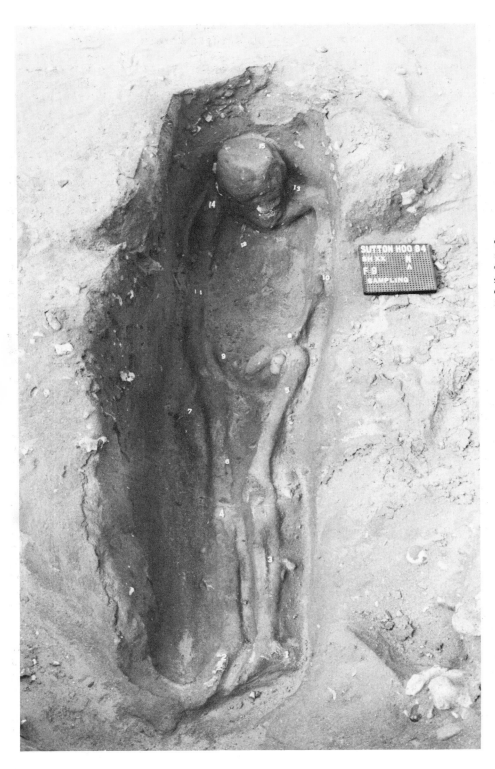

99 One of the
sand-bodies
excavated in 1984,
showing the
outline prepared
for sampling.

disturbed floor of a burial chamber. The burial party had dug a deep pit and within it built a chamber of vertically set overlapping oak planks. The burial was then laid out with the dead man placed in a flexed position in the south-west quadrant and his possessions, including a shield and drinking horns, in the eastern half. On top of the chamber they placed a 20m ship, not dissimilar to that in mound 1, whose stem and stern posts would have risen dramatically out of the mound. Mound 14, the robbed grave of a woman, contained the remains of a lightly built burial-chamber. The burial was virtually destroyed by grave robbers, whose trench could be seen cutting the east wall of the burial chamber. However enough evidence survived to show that this high-status woman had been buried in a coffin centrally placed in the chamber. A châtelaine, a small silver hinge, probably from a casket, and a silver buckle were amongst the possessions that were placed either in the coffin or around it.

Mound 17 proved to be the only high-status burial – apart from mound 1 – to survive intact. Two graves, one of a young man, the other of his pony, lay beneath a largely ploughed out mound. Excavation of the man's grave revealed possessions inside and outside the coffin and these were lifted by a team from the Department of Conservation in the British Museum. The major complexes consisted of a mass of iron and gilt-bronze fittings from the west end of the grave outside the oak coffin in which the princeling was placed and the pattern-welded sword that lay alongside him. A range of other possessions, placed outside the coffin, were also lifted. These included two spears and a shield boss, an iron-bound yew-wood tub, a copper-alloy bowl and a small cauldron with a grass-tempered pot inside it, a bone composite comb, and the remains of what may well be a leather satchel containing food.

The complex at the head of the grave was tentatively identified in the field as the pony's tack. After radiography of the block, excavation revealed a mass of iron that straddled the gilt-bronze fittings obscuring their relationship. More radiography revealed the clear outlines of a snaffle-bit and cheek-pieces with gilded copper-alloy fittings, all completely hidden within the corrosion products. Excavation of the block in the British Museum revealed a suite of gilt-bronze circular and axe-shaped fittings, with delicate leather straps surviving only in contact with the metal. Associated with the copper alloy mounts were sets of smaller fittings: one group contained three gilded bronze pendants or mounts, decorated with finely

modelled human masks between stylised bird heads, and two small gilded bronze mounts decorated with a simple twist; a pair of strap links each with a copper-alloy pendant in the form of a forked tail, decorated with plain silver sheet and two tiny gilded bird heads and two simple axe-shaped copper-alloy mounts covered with sheet silver.

The other major complex, the sword, looked a daunting prospect in the ground: iron corrosion obscured the hilt and the scabbard presented a fragile and flaking face to the archaeologists who surveyed it. But radiography revealed a group of scabbard fittings: a tiny silver buckle apparently associated with a copper-alloy scabbard slider inlaid with cloisonné garnet and ivory which lay horizontally across the scabbard. Associated with the slider was a copper-alloy sword pyramid, each face inlaid with garnets and a decayed setting. Analysis showed that these were also ivory. Beneath the sword lay a second 'pyramid' and a small triangular buckle covered with cloisonné cell-work of petal-like delicacy filled with garnets emphasised with settings of bright blue glass. Cabochon garnets concealing three rivets on the buckle-plate were originally set in ivory collars, showing that the buckle was clearly made *en suite* with the 'pyramids' and scabbard slider. While the assemblage is not as sumptuous as the gold and garnet sword fittings in mound 1, together with the horse harness, it confirms the high status of the young man.

The excavation was finally completed in April 1992 and assessment of the results is (1994) almost complete. The project established that the cemetery was small and raised over a complex prehistoric landscape. Burial within it, in the early seventh century, was probably restricted to high-ranking men, women and children within the sphere of the East Anglian ruling family. Its life was short, extending over only a few generations whose members lived and died during the late sixth and the first half of the seventh century, although the continuation of burial into the eighth century remains a possibility. The systematic emptying of the graves by robbers or antiquarians has prevented us from being certain of the status of the more complex burials – the inhumations in mounds 2 and 14 may well have approached mound 1 in the variety and quality of possessions that accompanied the dead man and woman. Whether they were royal or not is a question that may never be answered any more than the question of their relationship to the dead man in mound 1, or the perplexing question of why a cemetery of this status should have been placed on the very edges of the kingdom.

EAST ANGLIAN KINGS

THE WUFFINGAS

(Those who came to the throne are shown in black type.)

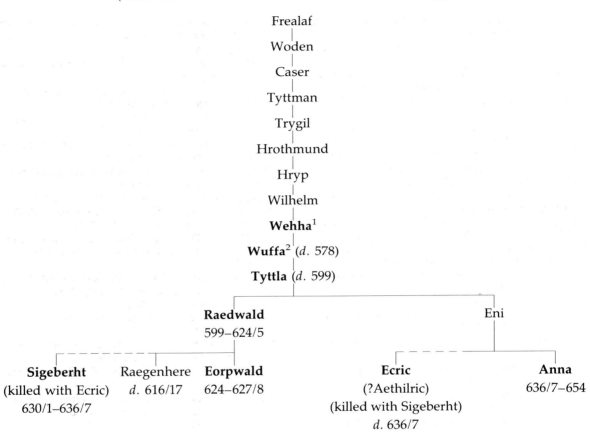

Frealaf

Woden

Caser

Tyttman

Trygil

Hrothmund

Hryp

Wilhelm

Wehha[1]

Wuffa[2] (*d.* 578)

Tyttla (*d.* 599)

Raedwald
599–624/5

Eni

Sigeberht
(killed with Ecric)
630/1–636/7

Raegenhere
d. 616/17

Eorpwald
624–627/8

Ecric
(?Aethilric)
(killed with Sigeberht)
d. 636/7

Anna
636/7–654

[1] 'The first to rule over the East Angles in Britain', according to a gloss against his name in the *Historia Brittonum*.
[2] Hence members of the kingly family were called Wuffingas.

Bibliography

ALCOCK, LESLIE, *Arthur's Britain, History and Archaeology A.D. 367–634* (London 1971).

ALEXANDER, M.R., *The Earliest English Poems* (London 1966).

BROWN, DAVID, 'The dating of the Sutton Hoo coins', *Anglo Saxon Studies in Archaeology and History*, 2, British Archaeological Report, British Series 92 (Oxford 1981).

BRUCE-MITFORD, RUPERT, *Aspects of Anglo-Saxon Archaeology* (London 1974).

BRUCE-MITFORD, RUPERT, *The Sutton Hoo Ship-Burial – a Handbook* (London 1947, 3rd ed. 1979).

BRUCE-MITFORD, RUPERT, *The Sutton Hoo Ship-Burial, Volume 1*, excavations, background, the ship, dating and inventory (London 1975).

BRUCE-MITFORD, RUPERT, *The Sutton Hoo Ship-Burial, Volume 2*, arms, armour and regalia (London 1978).

BRUCE-MITFORD, RUPERT, *The Sutton Hoo Ship-Burial, Volume 3*, silver, hanging-bowls, drinking-vessels, containers, musical instrument, textiles, minor objects (London 1983).

BRUCE-MITFORD, R. AND BRUCE-MITFORD, M., 'The Sutton Hoo lyre, Beowulf and the origins of the frame harp', *Antiquity* XLIV (1970) 7–13.

CAMPBELL, JAMES (ED.), *The Anglo-Saxons* (Oxford 1982).

CARVER, MARTIN, 'Project design', *Bulletin of the Sutton Hoo Research Committee* 4 (1986).

CARVER, MARTIN, (ED.), *The Age of Sutton Hoo*, The Boydell Press, 1992.

CARVER, MARTIN, (ED.), *Sutton Hoo Research Committee Bulletins*, The Boydell Press, 1993.

COLGRAVE, B. AND MYNORS, R.A.B. (EDS.), *Bede's Ecclesiastical History of the English People* (Oxford 1969).

CRAMP, ROSEMARY, 'Beowulf and Archaeology', *Medieval Archaeology* 1 (1977) 55–77.

CROSSLEY-HOLLAND, KEVIN, *Beowulf* (Cambridge 1968).

COUNCIL FOR BRITISH ARCHAEOLOGY, *Map of Saxon and Viking Britain*.

GLASS, SANDRA, 'The Sutton Hoo Ship-Burial', *Antiquity* XXXVI (1962) 179–93.

GRIERSON, PHILIP, 'The purpose of the Sutton Hoo coins', *Antiquity* XLIV (1970) 14–18.

GREEN, CHARLES, *Sutton Hoo, the Excavation of a Royal Burial Ship* (2nd ed., London 1968).

HOPE-TAYLOR, BRIAN, *Yeavering, an Anglo-British Centre of Early Northumbria* (London 1977).

HUNTER-BLAIR, PETER, *An Introduction to Anglo-Saxon England* (2nd ed., Cambridge 1978).

JAMES, EDWARD, *The Franks*, Basil Blackwell, 1988.

KENDRICK T.D. et al., 'The Sutton Hoo finds', *British Museum Quarterly* XIII (1938–9) 111–36.

KENT, J.P.C., 'Problems of chronology in the seventh century Merovingian coinage', *Cunobelin* XIII (1967) 24–30.

ORDNANCE SURVEY, *Map of Britain in the Dark Ages*.

PHILLIPS, C.W., 'The Sutton Hoo Ship-Burial', *Antiquaries Journal* XX (1940).

PHILLIPS, C.W. et al., 'The Sutton Hoo Ship-Burial', *Antiquity* XIV (1940).

SPEAKE, GEORGE, *Anglo-Saxon Animal Ornament and its Germanic Background* (Oxford 1980).

STENTON, F.M., *Anglo-Saxon England* (3rd ed., Oxford 1971).

WHITELOCK, D. (WITH D.C. DOUGLAS AND S.I. TUCKER), *The Anglo-Saxon Chronicle – a revised translation* (London 1961).

WILSON, D.M., *The Anglo-Saxons* (2nd ed., 1981).

WILSON, D.M., *Anglo-Saxon Art from the seventh century to the Norman Conquest* (London 1984).

WILSON, D.M. (ED.), *The Archaeology of Anglo-Saxon England* (London 1976).

Index